creating
a web page
with html

Visual QuickProject Guide

by Elizabeth Castro

Peachpit Press

Visual QuickProject Guide
Creating a Web Page with HTML
Elizabeth Castro

Peachpit Press
1249 Eighth Street
Berkeley, CA 94710
510/524-2178
800/283-9444
510/524-2221 (fax)

Find us on the World Wide Web at: www.peachpit.com
To report errors, please send a note to errata@peachpit.com
Peachpit Press is a division of Pearson Education

Cover design: Peachpit Press, Aren Howell
Cover production: Aren Howell
Interior design: Elizabeth Castro
Cover photo credit: Digital Vision

Notice of Liability
The information in this book is distributed on an "As Is" basis, without warranty. While every precaution has been taken in the preparation of the book, neither the author nor Peachpit Press shall have any liability to any person or entity with respect to any loss or damage caused or alleged to be caused directly or indirectly by the instructions contained in this book or by the computer software and hardware products described in it.

Trademarks
Visual QuickProject Guide is a registered trademark of Peachpit Press, a division of Pearson Education.

All other trademarks are the property of their respective owners.

Throughout this book, trademarks are used. Rather than put a trademark symbol with every occurrence of a trademarked name, we state that we are using the names in an editorial fashion only and to the benefit of the trademark owner with no intention of infringement of the trademark. No such use, or the use of any trade name, is intended to convey endorsement or other affiliation with this book.

ISBN 0-321-27847-X

9 8 7
Printed and bound in the United States of America

For Miquel and Rosa,
who got me started in this business
—and in Barcelona.

Special Thanks to...

Miquel Bada and Dimas Cabré, who lent me their offices,
computers, and Internet connections when I was
away from mine,

Margaret Christie, who looked through early drafts with
a beginner's eyes,

Lisa Brazieal and Connie Jeung-Mills at Peachpit Press,
who helped shepherd this book through production,

Nancy Davis, my amazing editor at Peachpit Press, who
continues to ask just the right questions and offer
just the right answers,

and Kissy Matthewson, who didn't want to learn so
much about HTML, and thus inspired this book.

contents

contents

introduction

The Visual QuickProject Guide that you hold in your hands offers a unique way to learn about new technologies. Instead of drowning you in theoretical possibilities and lengthy explanations, this Visual QuickProject Guide uses big, color illustrations coupled with clear, concise step-by-step instructions to show you how to complete one specific project in a matter of hours.

Our project in this book is to create a beautiful web site using HTML and CSS, the two fundamental and standard technologies used in web design today. Our web site showcases a collection of beautiful photographs and postcards, but since the project covers all the basic techniques, you'll be able to use what you learn to create your own web sites—perhaps to show off your vacation pictures from Egypt, share reading lists with your book group, or keep track of your team's soccer game schedule.

Why should you write your own HTML and CSS instead of using web page software like FrontPage or Dreamweaver? First, you can create HTML and CSS with the free text editor that came with your computer; no other investment is required. Second, HTML and CSS are simple and straightforward and easier to learn than a big software program. In addition, you'll have complete control over how your page looks and works. Finally, you'll be able to use the most standard and up-to-date versions of HTML and CSS, without waiting for—or paying for—software upgrades.

what you'll create

On the home page, create a transparent GIF image with beautiful text for a logo.

Use a background image that adds to the feel of your page (but doesn't distract from the content).

Create a navigation bar to give your page a distinctive look and make it easy for visitors to navigate your site.

Create links to other pages on your site.

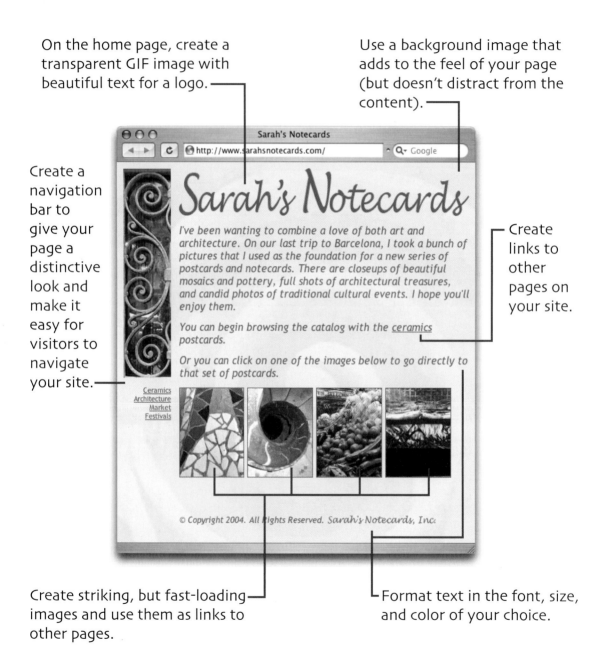

Create striking, but fast-loading images and use them as links to other pages.

Format text in the font, size, and color of your choice.

On the inner page, use headers to divide the information into hierarchical sections.

Format text to your liking.

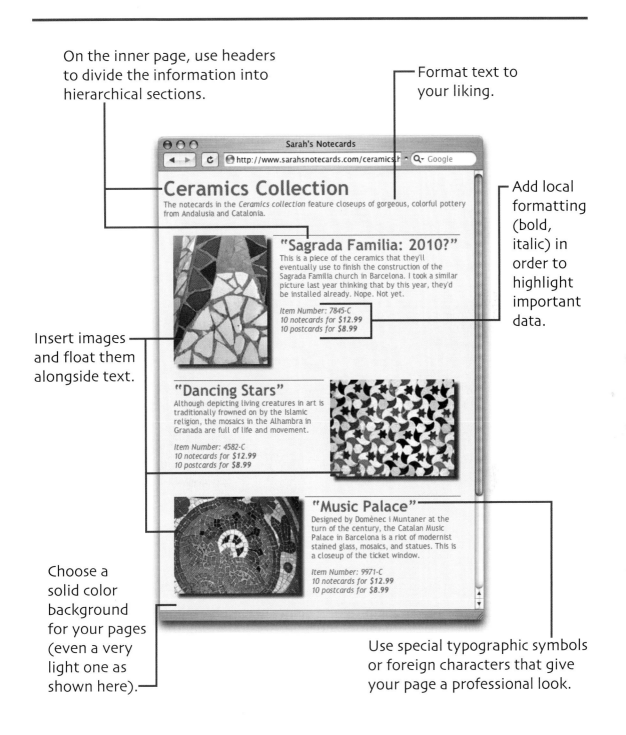

Add local formatting (bold, italic) in order to highlight important data.

Insert images and float them alongside text.

Choose a solid color background for your pages (even a very light one as shown here).

Use special typographic symbols or foreign characters that give your page a professional look.

Within the browser window:

Sarah's Notecards

http://www.sarahsnotecards.com/ceramics.h

Q▾ Google

Ceramics Collection

The notecards in the *Ceramics collection* feature closeups of gorgeous, colorful pottery from Andalusia and Catalonia.

"Sagrada Familia: 2010?"

This is a piece of the ceramics that they'll eventually use to finish the construction of the Sagrada Familia church in Barcelona. I took a similar picture last year thinking that by this year, they'd be installed already. Nope. Not yet.

Item Number: 7845-C
10 notecards for $12.99
10 postcards for $8.99

"Dancing Stars"

Although depicting living creatures in art is traditionally frowned on by the Islamic religion, the mosaics in the Alhambra in Granada are full of life and movement.

Item Number: 4582-C
10 notecards for $12.99
10 postcards for $8.99

"Music Palace"

Designed by Domènec i Muntaner at the turn of the century, the Catalan Music Palace in Barcelona is a riot of modernist stained glass, mosaics, and statues. This is a closeup of the ticket window.

Item Number: 9971-C
10 notecards for $12.99
10 postcards for $8.99

how this book works

The title of each section explains what is covered on that page.

In this book, you'll create two HTML files (ceramics.html in Chapter 1 and index.html in Chapter 2). The code that you'll need to type in for the HTML files will be displayed on an orange background.

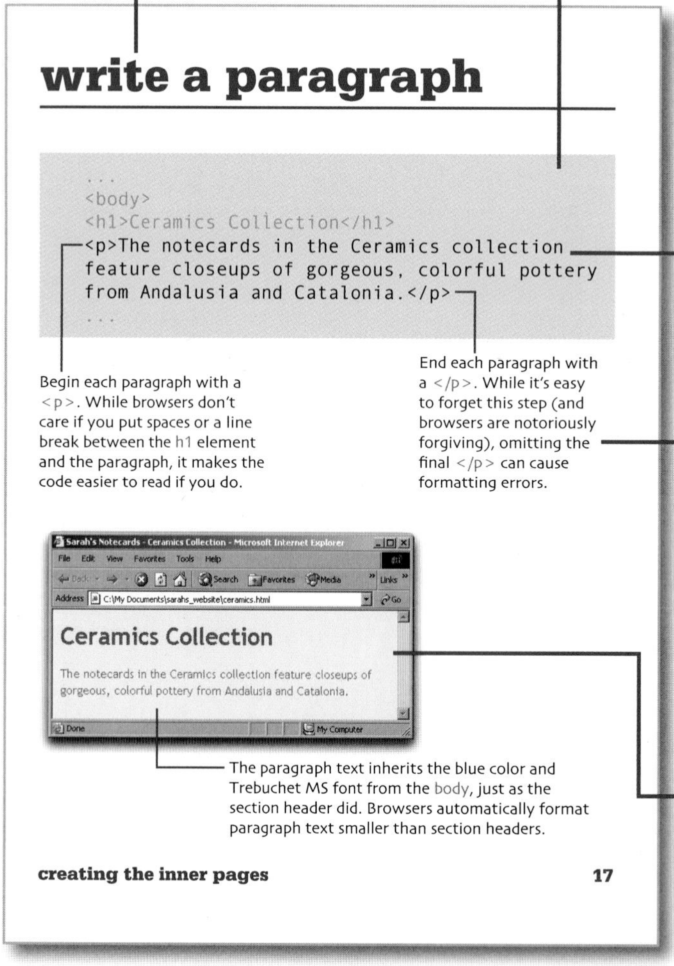

New code is in black while code from previous pages is in orange.

write a paragraph

```
...
<body>
<h1>Ceramics Collection</h1>
<p>The notecards in the Ceramics collection
feature closeups of gorgeous, colorful pottery
from Andalusia and Catalonia.</p>
...
```

Begin each paragraph with a <p>. While browsers don't care if you put spaces or a line break between the h1 element and the paragraph, it makes the code easier to read if you do.

End each paragraph with a </p>. While it's easy to forget this step (and browsers are notoriously forgiving), omitting the final </p> can cause formatting errors.

Captions explain what you're doing and why. They point to the relevant parts of the code.

Sarah's Notecards - Ceramics Collection - Microsoft Internet Explorer

File   Edit   View   Favorites   Tools   Help

Back · · · Search Favorites Media   Links

Address C:\My Documents\sarahs_website\ceramics.html   Go

Ceramics Collection

The notecards in the Ceramics collection feature closeups of gorgeous, colorful pottery from Andalusia and Catalonia.

Done   My Computer

The paragraph text inherits the blue color and Trebuchet MS font from the body, just as the section header did. Browsers automatically format paragraph text smaller than section headers.

A screenshot shows the effect of the new code in the browser.

creating the inner pages   **17**

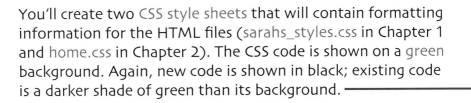
You'll create two CSS style sheets that will contain formatting information for the HTML files (sarahs_styles.css in Chapter 1 and home.css in Chapter 2). The CSS code is shown on a green background. Again, new code is shown in black; existing code is a darker shade of green than its background.

An ellipsis (...) indicates that there is more code in this document and that it was explained on an earlier page.

Names of HTML elements, CSS properties, file names, and other important concepts are shown in orange.

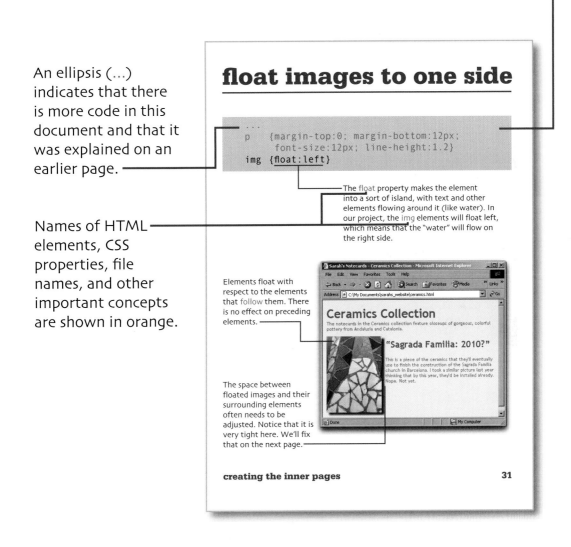

float images to one side

```
...
p    {margin-top:0; margin-bottom:12px;
      font-size:12px; line-height:1.2}
img  {float:left}
```

The float property makes the element into a sort of island, with text and other elements flowing around it (like water). In our project, the img elements will float left, which means that the "water" will flow on the right side.

Elements float with respect to the elements that follow them. There is no effect on preceding elements.

Sarah's Notecards - Ceramics Collection - Microsoft Internet Explorer

File Edit View Favorites Tools Help

Back ▾ ⇒ ▾ ⊗ ⊗ ⌂ | ⊗ Search ⊗ Favorites ⊗ Media | Links

Address C:\My Documents\sarahs_website\ceramics.html ▾ Go

Ceramics Collection

The notecards in the Ceramics collection feature closeups of gorgeous, colorful pottery from Andalusia and Catalonia.

"Sagrada Família: 2010?"

This is a piece of the ceramics that they'll eventually use to finish the construction of the Sagrada Família church in Barcelona. I took a similar picture last year thinking that by this year, they'd be installed already. Nope. Not yet.

Done | My Computer

The space between floated images and their surrounding elements often needs to be adjusted. Notice that it is very tight here. We'll fix that on the next page.

creating the inner pages   **31**

how this book works

The extra bits section at the end of each chapter contains additional tips and tricks that you might like to know—but that aren't absolutely necessary for creating the web page.

The heading for each group of tips matches the section title. (The colors are just for decoration and have no hidden meaning.)

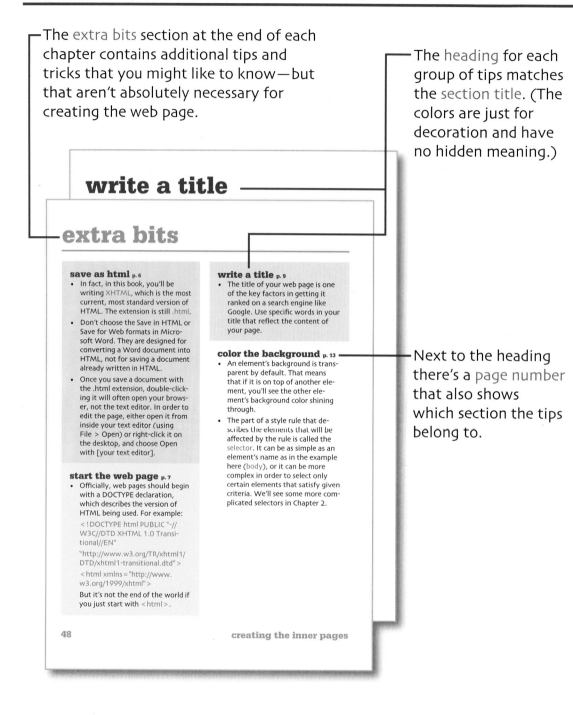

write a title

extra bits

save as html p. 6
- In fact, in this book, you'll be writing XHTML, which is the most current, most standard version of HTML. The extension is still .html.
- Don't choose the Save in HTML or Save for Web formats in Microsoft Word. They are designed for converting a Word document into HTML, not for saving a document already written in HTML.
- Once you save a document with the .html extension, double-clicking it will often open your browser, not the text editor. In order to edit the page, either open it from inside your text editor (using File > Open) or right-click it on the desktop, and choose Open with [your text editor].

start the web page p. 7
- Officially, web pages should begin with a DOCTYPE declaration, which describes the version of HTML being used. For example:

  <!DOCTYPE html PUBLIC "-//W3C//DTD XHTML 1.0 Transitional//EN"

  "http://www.w3.org/TR/xhtml1/DTD/xhtml1-transitional.dtd">

  <html xmlns="http://www.w3.org/1999/xhtml">

  But it's not the end of the world if you just start with <html>.

write a title p. 9
- The title of your web page is one of the key factors in getting it ranked on a search engine like Google. Use specific words in your title that reflect the content of your page.

color the background p. 13
- An element's background is transparent by default. That means that if it is on top of another element, you'll see the other element's background color shining through.
- The part of a style rule that describes the elements that will be affected by the rule is called the selector. It can be as simple as an element's name as in the example here (body), or it can be more complex in order to select only certain elements that satisfy given criteria. We'll see some more complicated selectors in Chapter 2.

Next to the heading there's a page number that also shows which section the tips belong to.

48   creating the inner pages

the web site

You can find this book's companion web site at http://www.cookwood.com/htmlvqj/

Be sure to visit the extras section, where you'll find a complete list of HTML elements, CSS properties, color codes, and much more.

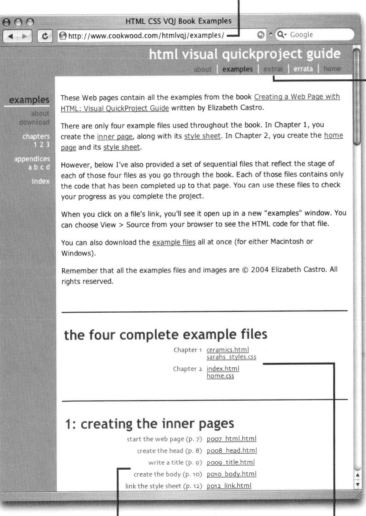

In the examples section of the companion site, you'll find the complete project files created in this book, including the image files, as well as the intermediate files created on each page.

useful tools

The most important tools for creating a web page are a computer and a text editor. It doesn't matter if your computer runs Windows, Unix, or Macintosh system software. While specialized text editors like BBEdit (shown) offer helpful tools for writing HTML and CSS, the free text editor that came with your computer—Notepad for Windows, TextEdit for Macintosh—will also work just fine.

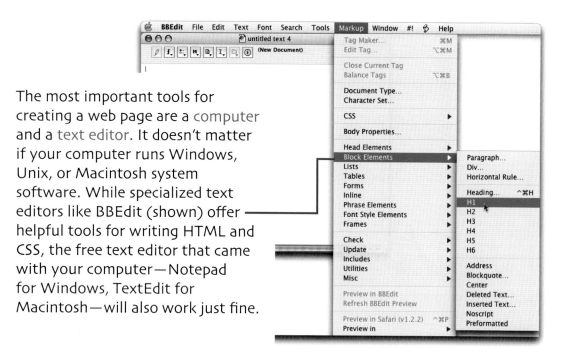

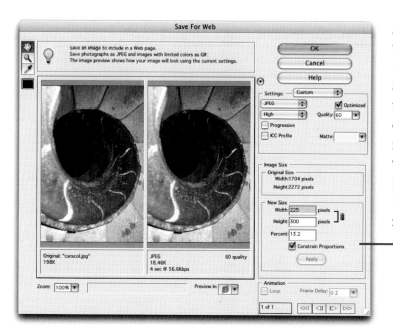

An image editor is useful for retouching and resizing photographs and graphic images for your web site. Many digital cameras and scanners come bundled with some kind of image editor, like Adobe Photoshop Elements, shown here.

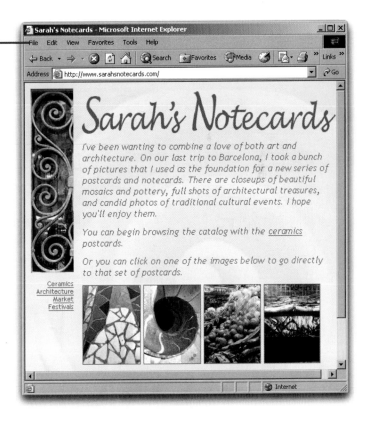

Once you've finished writing your web site you'll need to upload it to your web host to make it available on the Internet. While some web hosts let you do this through a browser, an FTP program, like Cute FTP (shown) makes transferring the files much easier.

And, of course, you'll want to use one or more browsers, like Internet Explorer (shown), Opera, and Safari, in order to test your pages and make sure they look the way they should. Explorer and Safari are both free. Opera has both a free and a paid version.

the next step

While this Visual QuickProject Guide will you give you an excellent foundation in HTML (actually XHTML) and CSS, I have to confess that there's a lot more to learn: tables, frames, forms, multimedia, and much more. If you're curious, check out my complete reference: HTML for the World Wide Web, with XHTML and CSS, Fifth Edition: Visual QuickStart Guide, also published by Peachpit Press.

The HTML VQS features clear examples, concise, step-by-step instructions, hundreds of illustrations, and lots of helpful tips. It covers every aspect of HTML (XHTML) and CSS in detail. It is the number one bestselling guide to HTML.

1. creating the inner pages

Ceramics Collection

The notecards in the *Ceramics collection* feature closeups of gorgeous, colorful pottery from Andalusia and Catalonia.

"Sagrada Familia: 2010?"

This is a piece of the ceramics that they'll eventually use to finish the construction of the Sagrada Familia church in Barcelona. I took a similar picture last year thinking that by this year, they'd be installed already. Nope. Not yet.

Item Number: 7845-C
10 notecards for $12.99
10 postcards for $8.99

"Dancing Stars"

Although depicting living creatures in art is traditionally frowned on by the Islamic religion, the mosaics in the Alhambra in Granada are full of life and movement.

Item Number: 4582-C
10 notecards for $12.99
10 postcards for $8.99

"Music Palace"

Designed by Domènec i Muntaner at the turn of the century, the Catalan Music Palace in Barcelona is a riot of modernist stained glass, mosaics, and statues. This is a closeup of the ticket window.

Item Number: 9971-C
10 notecards for $12.99
10 postcards for $8.99

The project that we'll complete in this book is a web site with two kinds of pages: inner pages that contain details and photos about the postcard collections that we sell, and one main, or home page which links to each of those individual pages. Because it's simpler, we'll start in this chapter by creating one of the inner pages, as shown at left. We'll create the home page in Chapter 2.

what we'll do

1 First, on pages 4–10, we'll get set up by creating a text file for the web page itself (ceramics.html). We'll then create its basic structure and give it a title.

3 On pages 14–18, we'll create the level 1 header and the first paragraph and select a font and color for both.

5 On pages 27–31, we'll move on to creating the level 2 headers and the additional text. We'll adjust the size of the new content and then float the image to its left.

7 On pages 35–38, we'll then add the item and price information with manual line breaks and local formatting.

9 On pages 42–47, we'll finally move on to adding the three other postcards on this page, and then we'll classify them so that every other one floats to the right.

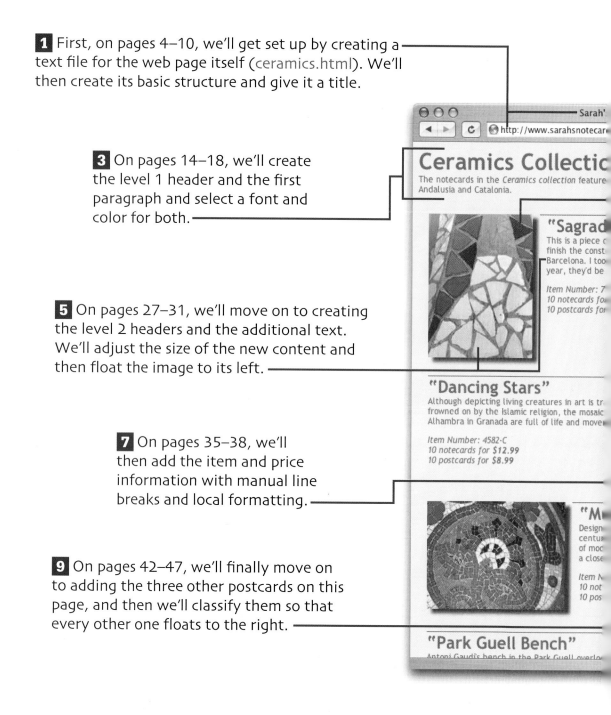

creating the inner pages

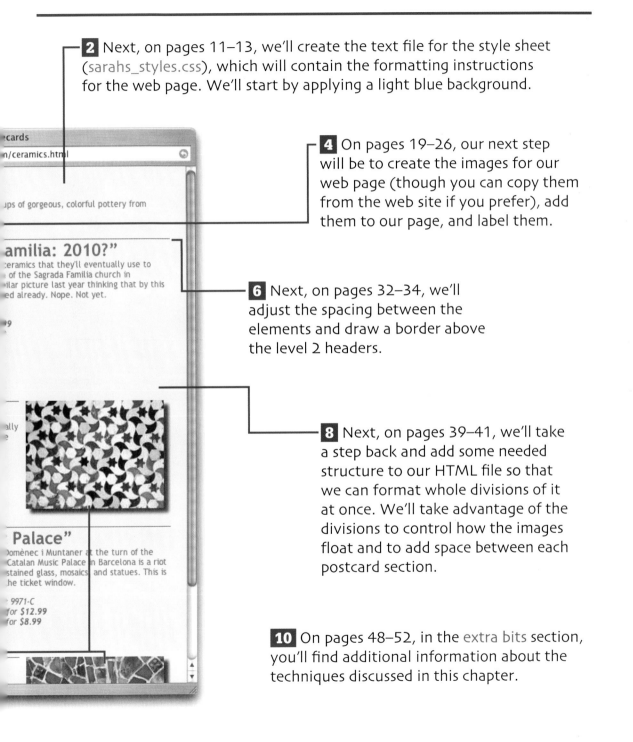

2 Next, on pages 11–13, we'll create the text file for the style sheet (sarahs_styles.css), which will contain the formatting instructions for the web page. We'll start by applying a light blue background.

4 On pages 19–26, our next step will be to create the images for our web page (though you can copy them from the web site if you prefer), add them to our page, and label them.

6 Next, on pages 32–34, we'll adjust the spacing between the elements and draw a border above the level 2 headers.

8 Next, on pages 39–41, we'll take a step back and add some needed structure to our HTML file so that we can format whole divisions of it at once. We'll take advantage of the divisions to control how the images float and to add space between each postcard section.

10 On pages 48–52, in the extra bits section, you'll find additional information about the techniques discussed in this chapter.

ecards
n/ceramics.html

ps of gorgeous, colorful pottery from

amilia: 2010?"
eramics that they'll eventually use to
of the Sagrada Familia church in
ilar picture last year thinking that by this
ed already. Nope. Not yet.

9

ally
e

Palace"
omènec i Muntaner at the turn of the
Catalan Music Palace in Barcelona is a riot
stained glass, mosaics and statues. This is
he ticket window.

9971-C
for $12.99
for $8.99

create a folder

In the Windows Explorer (as shown here) or in the Mac's Finder, choose File > New > Folder to create the folder in which you'll organize all the files in your web site. This simple, but extremely important, step will take all the pain out of creating links and inserting images later on.

Call the folder sarahs_website, with all lowercase letters. Never include spaces or any punctuation besides the underscore. (This is Mac OS X but the Windows desktop is pretty similar looking.)

creating the inner pages

open a new html file

A web page is nothing more than a simple text file. To start yours, choose File > New from your preferred text editor. You can use a dedicated text editor like Bare Bones Software's BBEdit (for Mac) or UltraEdit (for Windows) or a word processor like Word or WordPerfect.

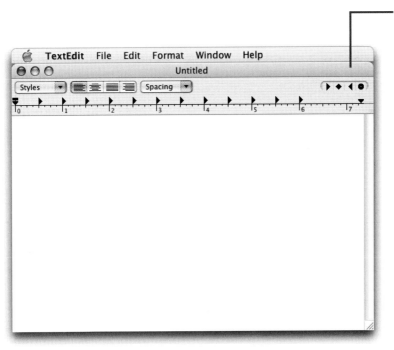

Here is a new, empty text document in TextEdit for Macintosh. You can use the text editor or word processor that you're most comfortable with (or that's the cheapest).

creating the inner pages

save as html

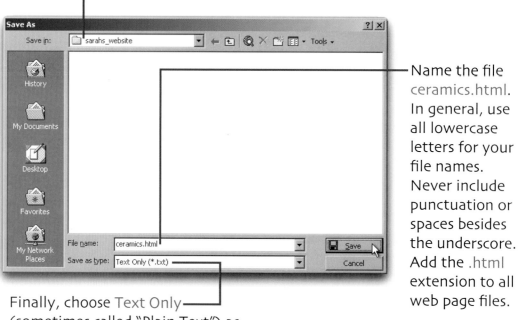

Before you start writing your web page, save it in the proper format by choosing File > Save As from your text editor or word processor.

It's absolutely essential that you pay attention to where you save your files. In this example, we'll save everything in the sarahs_website folder we created earlier.

Name the file ceramics.html. In general, use all lowercase letters for your file names. Never include punctuation or spaces besides the underscore. Add the .html extension to all web page files.

Finally, choose Text Only (sometimes called "Plain Text") as the format for your web page files.

start the web page

The `<html>` tag is the first bit of HTML code that you should type in the ceramics.html web page file that you created on the previous page. After leaving space for the contents of your web page, type the closing `</html>` tag.

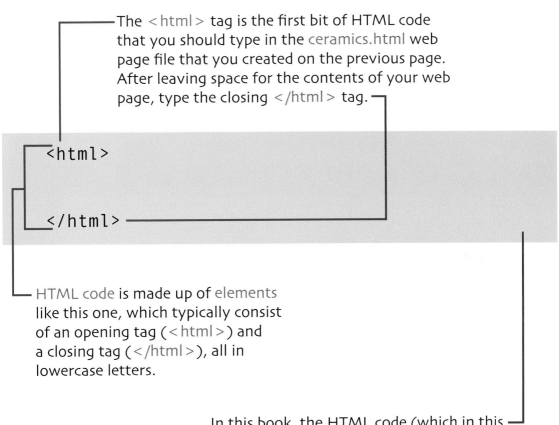

```
<html>


</html>
```

HTML code is made up of elements like this one, which typically consist of an opening tag (`<html>`) and a closing tag (`</html>`), all in lowercase letters.

In this book, the HTML code (which in this chapter is the contents of the ceramics.html file) will appear with a light orange background as shown here. The tags being discussed on a particular page will be shown in black while the existing tags (already explained on previous pages) will be shown in a slightly darker orange.

create the head

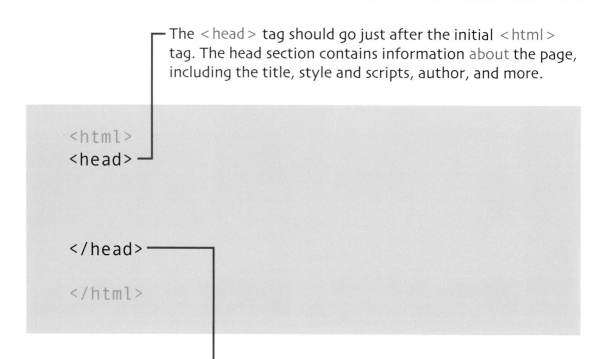

The < head > tag should go just after the initial < html > tag. The head section contains information about the page, including the title, style and scripts, author, and more.

```
<html>
<head>




</head>

</html>
```

The closing < /head > tag separates the information of the head section from the contents of the body section (which contains the visible part of your web page, and which we'll create on page 10).

write a title

The title of your page goes inside opening and closing title tags within the head section of your web page file. It doesn't matter if the code spans more than one line.

```
<html>
<head>
<title>Sarah's Notecards - Ceramics Collection
</title>

</head>
. . .
```

In this book, the ellipsis (...) indicates that there is more code than can fit in the illustration.

The title is displayed in the browser's window bar (often with the browser's name).

Sarah's Notecards - Ceramics Collection - Microsoft Internet Explorer	_ □ ×

| File | Edit | View | Favorites | Tools | Help |

| ⇐ Back ▾ ⇒ ▾ | | | | | Media | | » | Links » |

| Address | C:\My D | | | | | ▾ | Go |

Add to Favorites...
Organize Favorites...

📁 Cookwood Crawler Page ▸
📁 Links ▸
🖹 Software Updates ▸
🖹 Sarah's Notecards - Ceramics Collection

| Done | | 💻 My Computer |

Titles are also used by default to identify pages saved as favorites or bookmarks.

create the body

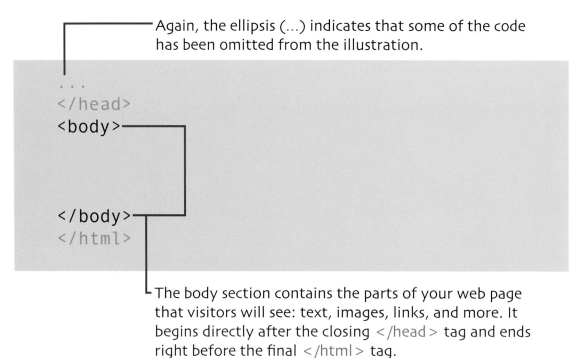

Again, the ellipsis (...) indicates that some of the code has been omitted from the illustration.

```
...
</head>
<body>

</body>
</html>
```

The body section contains the parts of your web page that visitors will see: text, images, links, and more. It begins directly after the closing </head> tag and ends right before the final </html> tag.

create the style sheet

1 A style sheet is a separate text file that contains the formatting instructions for your web page. To create one, choose File > New from your preferred text editor.

2 Next, choose File > Save As to give the style sheet the proper name and extension.

3 Use sarahs_styles.css for the name of the style sheet. In general, use all lowercase letters with no punctuation or spaces except the underscore, and always add the .css extension.

4 Again, pay attention to where you save your files. For this project, we'll store everything in the sarahs_website folder to facilitate linking the documents later.

5 Be sure to save the style sheet in Plain Text or Text Only format. Accept the default encoding.

link the style sheet

The link tag can be placed anywhere between the opening and closing head tags (in the HTML file).

In this book, you'll learn how to create CSS or Cascading Style Sheets. While there are other style sheet languages, CSS is the standard.

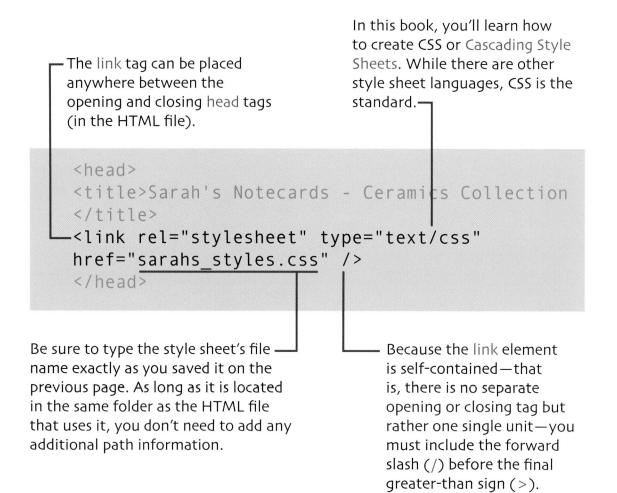

```
<head>
<title>Sarah's Notecards - Ceramics Collection
</title>
<link rel="stylesheet" type="text/css"
href="sarahs_styles.css" />
</head>
```

Be sure to type the style sheet's file name exactly as you saved it on the previous page. As long as it is located in the same folder as the HTML file that uses it, you don't need to add any additional path information.

Because the link element is self-contained—that is, there is no separate opening or closing tag but rather one single unit—you must include the forward slash (/) before the final greater-than sign (>).

color the background

The actual formatting instructions consist of a property (background) and value (#EDF2FF, which is the CSS way to specify the blue I wanted) separated by a colon (:). You can find a table of CSS properties and values in Appendix B. You'll find a color chart in Appendix C.

This will be the first line of the sarahs_styles.css style sheet that we created on page 11.

```
body {background: #EDF2FF}
```

A style rule begins with the name of the element(s) that you are formatting (body, in this case) and is followed by curly brackets ({ }) that contain the details about how the element should be styled.

In this book, the code for style sheets (which in this chapter is the contents of the sarahs_styles.css file) will be shown with a green background. The new code being discussed will be shown in black while existing fragments will be shown in a darker green.

Save both the CSS and the HTML files and then open the web page with a browser to see the blue background.

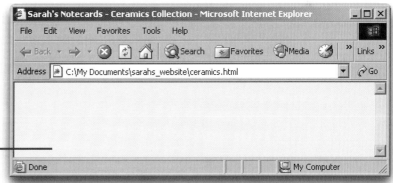

creating the inner pages

add a section header

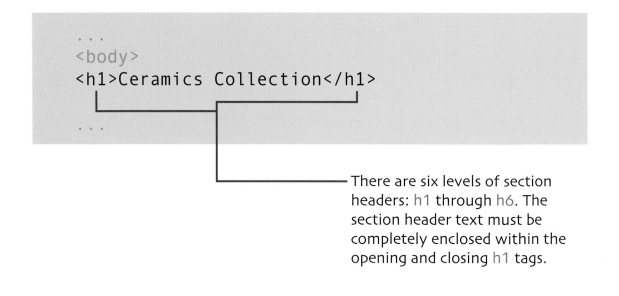

```
. . .
<body>
<h1>Ceramics Collection</h1>


. . .
```

There are six levels of section headers: h1 through h6. The section header text must be completely enclosed within the opening and closing h1 tags.

Sarah's Notecards – Ceramics Collection

file:///Users/liz/Documents/sarahs_website/ Google

Ceramics Collection

Browsers generally format an h1 header in black 24-point Times, with lots of space above and below (yech!).

choose fonts

Each style rule may have as many property-value pairs as needed. Separate each one from the next with a semicolon (;).

Enclose multi-word font names in quotes (").

Separate font choices with commas (,).

```
body {background: #EDF2FF;
      font-family: "Trebuchet MS", Arial,
         Helvetica, sans-serif}
```

Some properties (like font-family) are inherited. This means that they affect not only the element to which they are applied (body) but also the elements contained in that element (h1). Appendix B explains which properties are inherited.

The font-family property lets you specify the preferred fonts for displaying a given element. If the first font is not available on your visitor's computer, the second font will be attempted, and so on. You can also specify a generic font style (like sans-serif) in case the visitor has none of the preferred fonts installed.

After saving the CSS file and refreshing the browser, you can see the new font (in this case, the visitor's computer did have Trebuchet MS, a pretty common font, installed). We'll work on the color and spacing shortly.

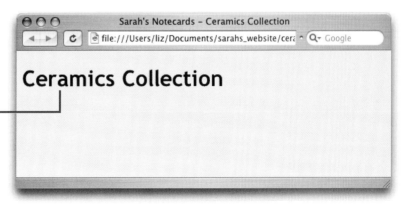

change text color

```
body {background: #EDF2FF;
      font-family: "Trebuchet MS", Arial,
      Helvetica, sans-serif;
      color: #4D65A0}
```

The color property controls the "foreground" color of an element. It's principally used to change text color. You'll find a list of allowed color names, as well as a selection of colors and their codes, in Appendix C.

Text on a web page looks best when there's enough contrast between it and the background. You don't want to make your visitors have to strain to read your page.

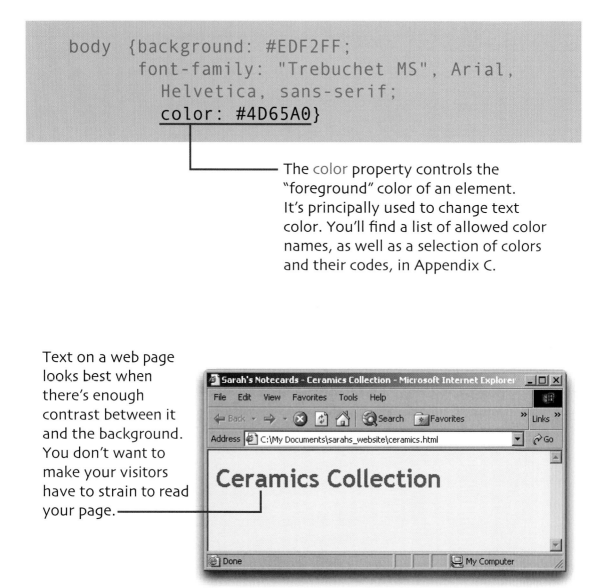

write a paragraph

```
. . .
<body>
<h1>Ceramics Collection</h1>
<p>The notecards in the Ceramics collection
feature closeups of gorgeous, colorful pottery
from Andalusia and Catalonia.</p>
. . .
```

Begin each paragraph with a <p>. While browsers don't care if you put spaces or a line break between the h1 element and the paragraph, it makes the code easier to read if you do.

End each paragraph with a </p>. While it's easy to forget this step (and browsers are notoriously forgiving), omitting the final </p> can cause formatting errors.

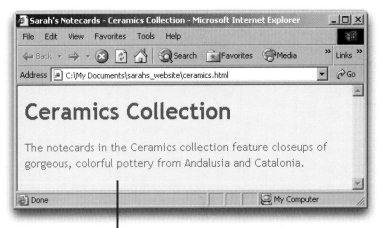

The paragraph text inherits the blue color and Trebuchet MS font from the body, just as the section header did. Browsers automatically format paragraph text smaller than section headers.

adjust spacing

```
body {background: #EDF2FF;
      font-family: "Trebuchet MS", Arial,
      Helvetica, sans-serif;
      color: #4D65A0}
h1  {margin:0}
p   {margin-top:0; margin-bottom:12px}
```

The margin property controls how much space is added between elements. Most browsers automatically add margin space to headers and paragraphs. To keep the header section next to the paragraph that follows it, set margins for both elements to 0 (zero).

To keep a certain amount of space between paragraphs, set the bottom margin to 12 pixels, as shown. Make sure there is no space between the 12 and the px.

The section header looks much better closer to the paragraph. Note that the body still has a bit of margin which is keeping the h1 and p elements from butting up next to the browser window itself.

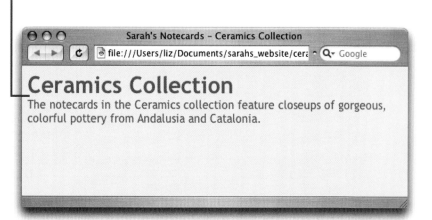

Sarah's Notecards – Ceramics Collection

file:///Users/liz/Documents/sarahs_website/cera   Q⫶ Google

Ceramics Collection
The notecards in the Ceramics collection feature closeups of gorgeous, colorful pottery from Andalusia and Catalonia.

create a web image

Here is the original photo, taken with a Canon G2 digital camera, at 2272 by 1704 pixels. The photo has an overall bluish tint and it seems like it could be cropped better. It's also huge, weighing in at 11Mb, which would take an awful long time to load.

The final image, which has been cropped and resized, had its levels adjusted, and saved as a compressed JPEG. It now takes up only 14.5K. There are many good image editors, including Adobe Photoshop Elements and JASC's Paint Shop Pro, which both retail for $99 but often come included free with digital cameras and scanners.

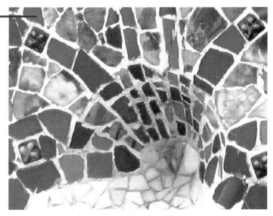

crop an image

1 Select the cropping tool. (This is Photoshop Elements but most image editors work in a similar way.)

2 If you want, set the desired final size in pixels. This saves you the job of resizing it manually later on.

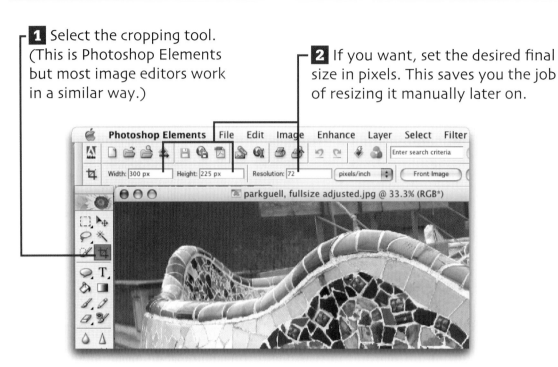

3 Position the cropping frame until the highlighted part covers just the portion of the image that you want to keep. Then double-click inside to crop (or choose Image > Crop).

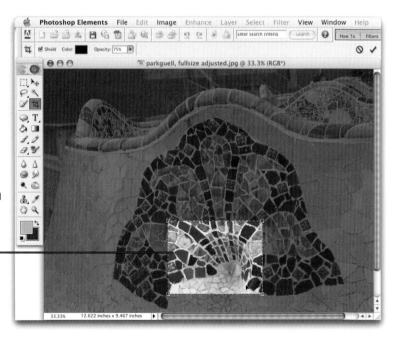

creating the inner pages

adjust levels

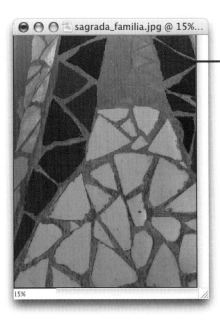

1 The original image is dark and lifeless.

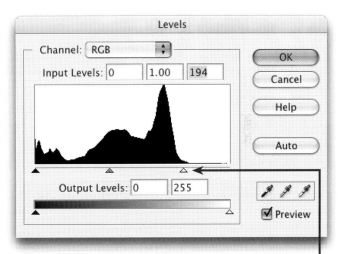

2 In the Levels box (Command - L), drag the white triangle leftward towards the foot of the mountain to increase the tonal range of the highlights. You can also drag the black triangle rightward toward the mountain (to adjust the shadows). Here it's not necessary.

3 The image is brighter and better balanced. The effect is even more pronounced (and important) on screen, i.e., in a web browser.

resize an image

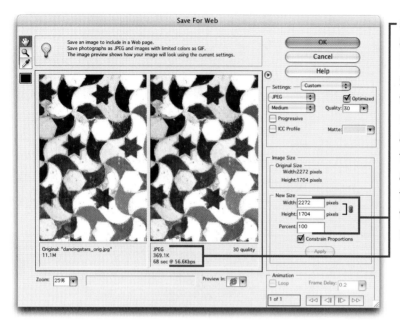

Many digital cameras and scanners create images that are simply too big for a web page. This one measures 2272 pixels across, almost four times as big as an average page. And it takes up 369K, which will take more than a minute to download.

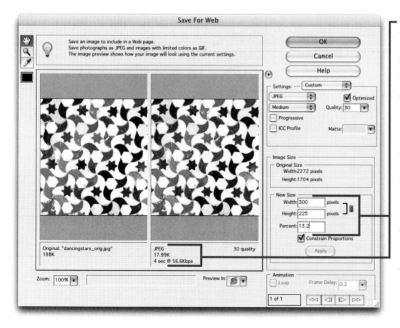

In Photoshop Elements, choose File > Save for Web and then use the Image Size area to resize your image. Choose a size keeping in mind that an average web page measures around 600 pixels wide, and that the bigger the image, the longer it will take to download. Here I've reduced the image to 300 pixels wide and it now only takes 4 seconds to download.

creating the inner pages

format photos as jpeg

The JPEG format is the most efficient compression system for photographs. ─

The Quality of the JPEG compression is directly related to the final size of the image. However, you can often trade a small amount of quality for a considerable amount of reduced download time. ─

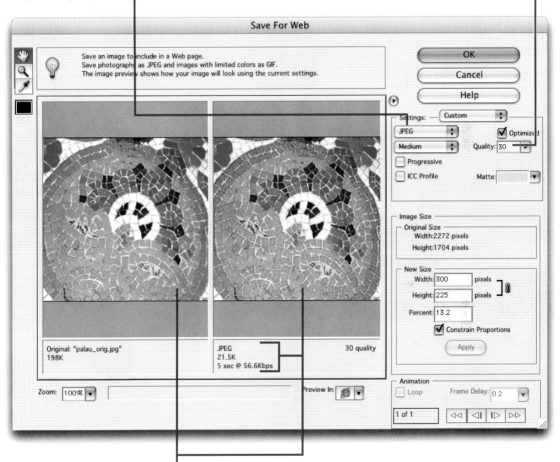

In Photoshop Elements' Save For Web dialog box, you can compare the compressed version with the original in order to determine a quality that's high enough to look pretty and low enough to ensure an acceptable download time.

organize the photos

Once you click OK in the Save For Web dialog box, you'll be able to give your image a name. Remember to use all lowercase letters and no spaces or punctuation except the underscore.

Pay attention to where you save your images. It's easiest if you put them in the same folder as your other web files.

When you've finished preparing your images, check again to make sure they're in the same folder as your HTML document. It will make linking the images much easier.

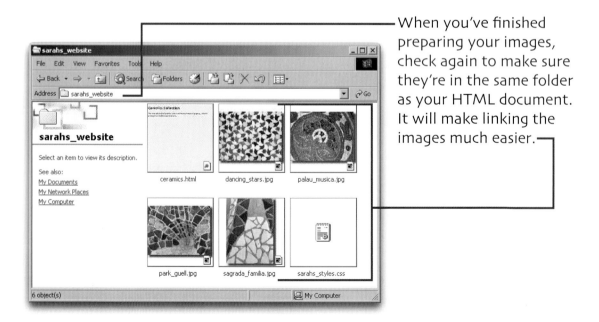

add photos to page

The img element is for adding photos to the page. Specify the image's file name and location with the src attribute. As long as the image is in the same folder as the HTML file, you don't need to add any extra path information.

The text in the alt attribute will appear if the image fails to load. It is also helpful to the vision impaired.

```
. . .
<p>The notecards in the Ceramics collection
feature closeups of gorgeous, colorful pottery
from Andalusia and Catalonia.</p>
<img src="sagrada_familia.jpg" alt="Future
Sagrada Familia Ceramics" width="160"
height="210" />
. . .
```

Type in the height and width of the image in pixels or as a percentage of the browser window.

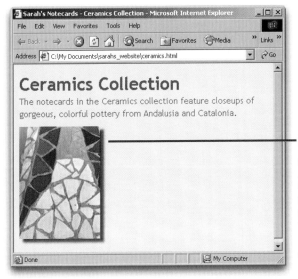

By default, an image appears directly after the code that precedes it. Since the preceding element was a paragraph, this image starts on its own line. Images, can, however, appear within a line.

label a photo

```
. . .
<img src="sagrada_familia.jpg" alt="Future
Sagrada Familia Ceramics" width="160"
height="210" title="Sagrada Familia: 2010?,
10 notecards for $12.99, 10 postcards for
$8.99" />
. . .
```

To create a label, insert a title attribute within the img element (it doesn't matter where). Be sure to enclose the label text in quotation marks.

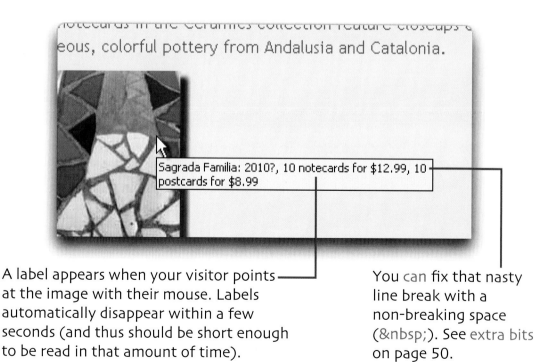

A label appears when your visitor points at the image with their mouse. Labels automatically disappear within a few seconds (and thus should be short enough to be read in that amount of time).

You can fix that nasty line break with a non-breaking space ( ). See extra bits on page 50.

add a subheader

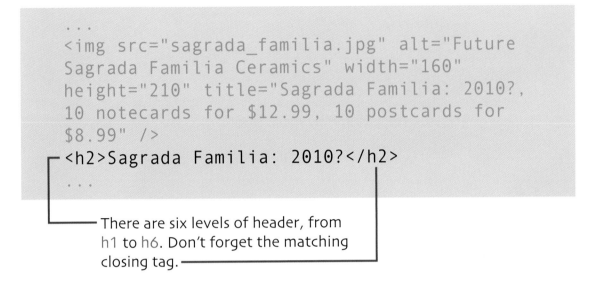

```
. . .
<img src="sagrada_familia.jpg" alt="Future
Sagrada Familia Ceramics" width="160"
height="210" title="Sagrada Familia: 2010?,
10 notecards for $12.99, 10 postcards for
$8.99" />
<h2>Sagrada Familia: 2010?</h2>
. . .
```

There are six levels of header, from h1 to h6. Don't forget the matching closing tag.

Headers automatically start on a new line.

Browsers automatically format headers bigger and bolder than surrounding text with each subsequent level smaller than the preceding one. The font and color that we applied to the entire body (on pages 15–16) override the browser's defaults.

use special characters

```
. . .
<h2>&ldquo;Sagrada Familia: 2010?&rdquo;</h2>
. . .
```

The code for a special character, called a reference, starts with an ampersand (&), which is followed by the character's name or number (ldquo), and is then finished off with a semicolon (;).

ldquo and rdquo stand for "left double quotes" and "right double quotes" respectively.

"Sagrada Familia: 2010?"

Done

Curly quotes and accents are among the most common special symbols that need to be entered with character references. They help give your page a professional look. If you type them in directly, they are not displayed properly. You can find a list of special characters and their corresponding references in Appendix D.

add more text

```
. . .
<h2>&ldquo;Sagrada Familia: 2010?&rdquo;</h2>
<p>This is a piece of the ceramics that
they'll eventually use to finish the
construction of the Sagrada Familia church
in Barcelona. I took a similar picture last
year thinking that by this year, they'd be
installed already. Nope. Not yet.</p>
. . .
```

Begin each paragraph with a `<p>`.

End each paragraph with a `</p>`.

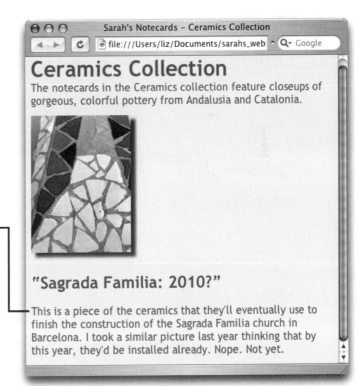

A new paragraph starts on its own line below the header. It has the same formatting as the first paragraph we entered.

change font size

There must be a semicolon between every property-value pair!

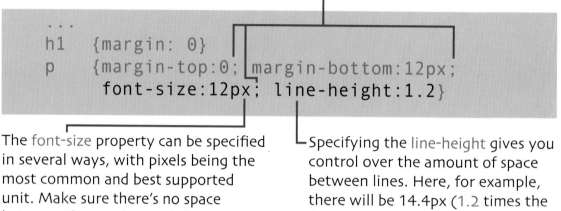

```
...
h1    {margin: 0}
p     {margin-top:0; margin-bottom:12px;
       font-size:12px; line-height:1.2}
```

The font-size property can be specified in several ways, with pixels being the most common and best supported unit. Make sure there's no space between the number and the px.

Specifying the line-height gives you control over the amount of space between lines. Here, for example, there will be 14.4px (1.2 times the font size of 12px) between each line of paragraph text.

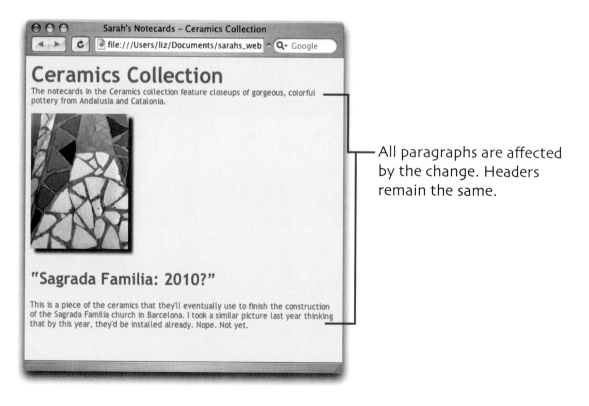

All paragraphs are affected by the change. Headers remain the same.

float images to one side

```
. . .
p     {margin-top:0; margin-bottom:12px;
       font-size:12px; line-height:1.2}
img  {float:left}
```

The float property makes the element into a sort of island, with text and other elements flowing around it (like water). In our project, the img elements will float left, which means that the "water" will flow on the right side.

Elements float with respect to the elements that follow them. There is no effect on preceding elements.

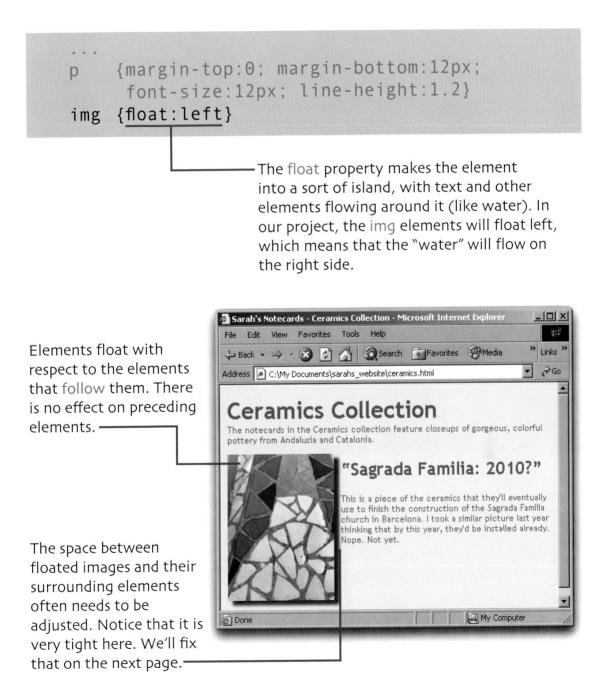

The space between floated images and their surrounding elements often needs to be adjusted. Notice that it is very tight here. We'll fix that on the next page.

pad the images

```
  . . .
p    {margin-top:0; margin-bottom:12px;
      font-size:12px; line-height:1.2}
img {float:left; padding-right:10px}
```

We'll add a 10-pixel-wide pad (a beach for our island) to the right side of the floating images to keep the surrounding elements from touching. Padding may also be applied to the top, bottom, or left, or to all sides (by leaving out the direction).

The text looks much better now that it is not jammed up next to the photo.

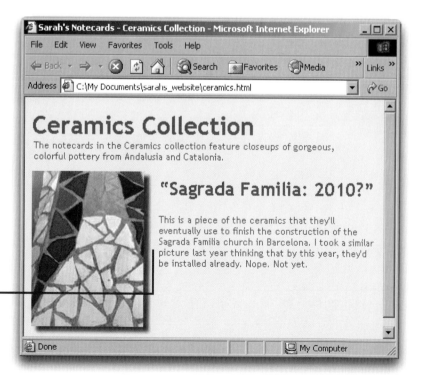

creating the inner pages

reuse styles

```
...
h1, h2    {margin: 0}
p         {margin-top:0; margin-bottom:12px;
           font-size:12px; line-height:1.2}
img       {float:left; padding-right:10px}
```

We applied a margin of 0 to the level 1 headers back on page 18 to remove the default space that most browsers apply around headers. To apply this style to level 2 headers as well, simply type a comma (,) and h2 after the original h1.

Ceramics Collection

Sarah's Notecards – Ceramics Collection

file:///Users/liz/Documents/sarahs_we   Google

Ceramics Collection

The notecards in the Ceramics collection feature closeups of gorgeous, colorful pottery from Andalusia and Catalonia.

"Sagrada Familia: 2010?"

This is a piece of the ceramics that they'll eventually use to finish the construction of the Sagrada Familia church in Barcelona. I took a similar picture last year thinking that by this year, they'd be installed already. Nope. Not yet.

I'm not sure why browsers habitually put so much space between a header and the paragraph that follows it. But it sure looks better now that we've gotten rid of the extra space.

draw a border

```
. . .
h1, h2      {margin: 0}
h2          {border-top: 1px solid #4D65A0}
p           {margin-top:0; margin-bottom:12px;
             font-size:12px; line-height:1.2}
. . .
```

Since we only want the level 2 headers to have the border, we make a new rule just for h2. Its properties will be added to previous rules that apply to h2 (and would override them if they conflicted—which here they do not).

A border has three parts: width (1px), style (solid), and color (#4D65A0). You'll find a list of border properties in Appendix B. You'll find a list of color codes in Appendix C.

"Sagrada Familia: 2010?"

This is a piece of the ceramics that they'll eventually use to finish the construction of the Sagrada Familia church in Barcelona. I took a similar picture last year thinking that by this year, they'd be installed already. Nope. Not yet.

A solid blue, 1-pixel border will now appear at the top of each level 2 header. Borders are drawn on the outside edge of any padding that has been applied and on the inside edge of the element's margin.

classify paragraphs

```
...
<p>This is a piece of the ceramics that
they'll eventually use to finish the
construction of the Sagrada Familia church
in Barcelona. I took a similar picture last
year thinking that by this year, they'd be
installed already. Nope. Not yet.</p>
<p class="sales_info">Item Number: 7845-C</p>
...
```

We'll create a new kind of paragraph for the postcards' sales information. We label these paragraphs as such by adding the class attribute. On the next page, we'll be able to add formatting to only the paragraphs labeled with this class.

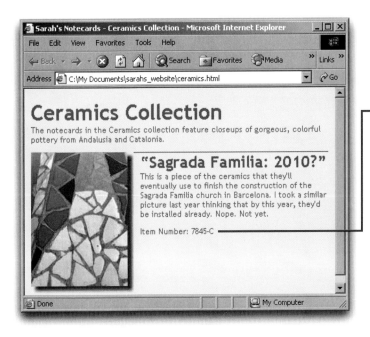

The sales_info paragraph starts out with the same formatting as all other paragraphs. We'll add to it on the next page.

apply italics to a class

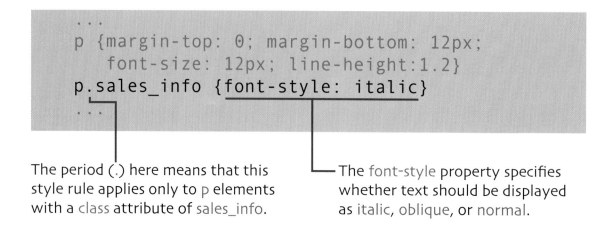

```
. . .
p {margin-top: 0; margin-bottom: 12px;
    font-size: 12px; line-height:1.2}
p.sales_info {font-style: italic}
. . .
```

The period (.) here means that this style rule applies only to p elements with a class attribute of sales_info.

The font-style property specifies whether text should be displayed as italic, oblique, or normal.

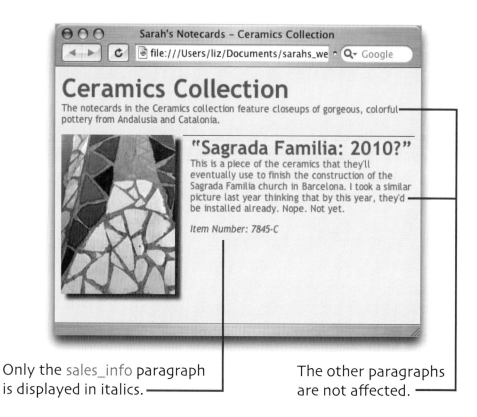

Only the sales_info paragraph is displayed in italics.

The other paragraphs are not affected.

add line breaks

```
. . .
<p class="sales_info">Item Number: 7845-C
<br />10 notecards for $12.99
<br />10 postcards for $8.99

</p>
. . .
```

Insert < br /> where each line break should occur. There should be a space between the br and the forward slash (/).

It doesn't matter if you type the HTML code on separate lines or not. I have done that here to make the code easier to read, but it is not required.

You might want to insert line breaks in short lists of things or in lines of poetry.

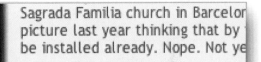

Sagrada Familia church in Barcelor
picture last year thinking that by
be installed already. Nope. Not ye

Item Number: 7845-C
10 notecards for $12.99
10 postcards for $8.99

add local formatting

Add `<i>` at the beginning and `</i>` at the end of text to display a small amount of text in italics. (For large amounts, use font-style, described on page 36.)

```
. . .
<p>The notecards in the <i>Ceramics collec-
tion</i> feature closeups of gorgeous, color-
ful pottery from Andalusia and Catalonia.</p>
. . .
<p class="sales_info">Item Number: 7845-C
<br />10 notecards for <b>$12.99</b>
<br />10 postcards for <b>$8.99</b>
. . .
```

Add `<b>` at the beginning and `</b>` at the end to make a small amount of text bold. (For large amounts, use font-weight, described on page 72.)

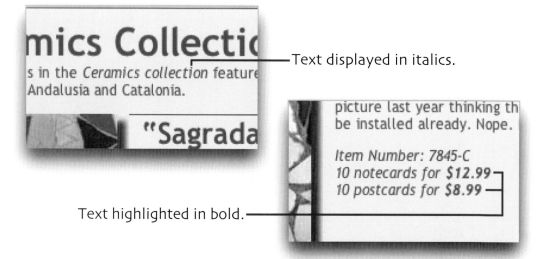

Text displayed in italics.

Text highlighted in bold.

add structure

We can divide the web page into its structural elements (introduction, information about postcards, etc.) with div elements, and then format those divisions as a unit (as shown on pages 40–41).

Label each division with an appropriate value for the class attribute (e.g., intro and postcard).

```
...
<div class="intro"><h1>Ceramics Collection
</h1>
<p>The notecards in the <i>Ceramics collec-
tion</i> feature closeups of gorgeous, color-
ful pottery from Andalusia and Catalonia.</p>
</div>

<div class="postcard">
<img src="sagrada_familia.jpg" alt="Sagrada
Familia Ceramics" width="160" height="210"
title= "Sagrada Familia: 2010?, 10 notecards
for $12.99, 10 postcards for $8.99" />

<h2>&ldquo;Sagrada Familia: 2010?&rdquo;</h2>
<p>This is a piece of the ceramics that ...
Nope. Not yet.</p>

<p class="sales_info">Item Number: 7845-C
<br />10 notecards for <b>$12.99</b>
<br />10 postcards for <b>$8.99</b>
</p>
</div>
...
```

pad a division

Once we have created and labeled the divisions of our web page, we can apply styles to an entire division. Here we add 15 pixels of padding around all four sides of each postcard division.

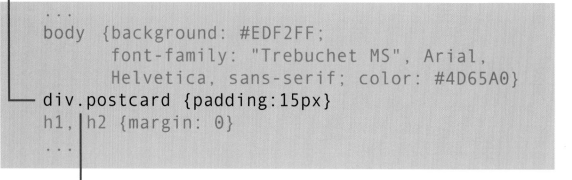

```
. . .
body {background: #EDF2FF;
      font-family: "Trebuchet MS", Arial,
      Helvetica, sans-serif; color: #4D65A0}
div.postcard {padding:15px}
h1, h2 {margin: 0}
. . .
```

Remember, the period means "apply this style to only the div elements whose class is postcard".

The postcard division (but not the intro division) now has 15 pixels of padding on all sides to help set it off from the other parts of the web page.

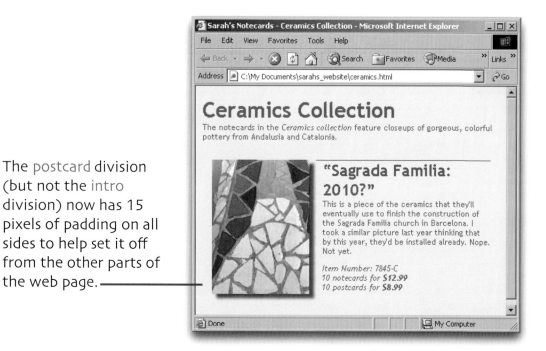

creating the inner pages

clear floats

Set the clear property for div elements to both so that a new postcard division (which we'll add on pages 42–43) won't start until both the left and right sides are free of floating elements—that is, until we get past the picture of the previous postcard.

```
...
body {background: #EDF2FF;
      font-family: "Trebuchet MS", Arial,
      Helvetica, sans-serif; color: #4D65A0}
div {clear:both}
div.postcard {padding:15px}
h1, h2 {margin: 0}
...
```

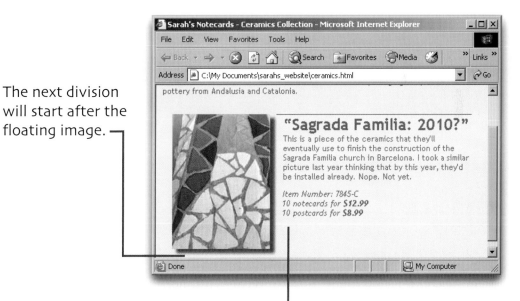

The next division will start after the floating image.

Without the clear property, the next elements would start directly after the preceding element (10 postcards for $8.99).

add another postcard

The new division has precisely the same elements as the previous one: an image with a title followed by a level 2 header, a paragraph, and finally, the sales information.

```
. . .
<p class="sales_info">Ref: 7845-C
<br />10 notecards for <b>$12.99</b>
<br />10 postcards for <b>$8.99</b>
</p>
</div>
<div class="postcard">
<img src="dancing_stars.jpg" alt="Dancing
Stars at the Alhambra" width="210"
height="160" title="Alhambra Stars, 10
notecards for $12.99, 10 postcards for
$8.99" />
<h2>&ldquo;Dancing Stars&rdquo;</h2>
<p>Although depicting living creatures in art
is traditionally frowned on by the Islamic
religion, the mosaics in the Alhambra in
Granada are full of life and movement.
</p>

<p class="sales_info">Item Number: 4582-C
<br />10 notecards for <b>$12.99</b>
<br />10 postcards for <b>$8.99</b>
</p>
</div>
```

The beauty of CSS is that the new elements are automatically formatted just like their existing counterparts.

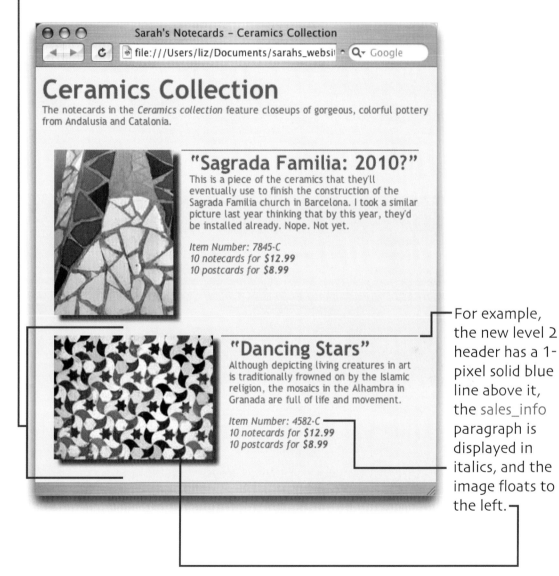

For example, the new level 2 header has a 1-pixel solid blue line above it, the sales_info paragraph is displayed in italics, and the image floats to the left.

float images to right

```
...
<div class="postcard">
<img src="sagrada_familia.jpg" class="odd"
alt="Sagrada Familia Ceramics" width="160"
height="210" title= "Sagrada Familia: 2010?,
10 notecards for $12.99, 10 postcards for
$8.99" />


...
<div class="postcard">
<img src="dancing_stars.jpg" class="even"
alt="Dancing Stars at the Alhambra"
width="210" height="160" title="Alhambra
Stars, 10 notecards for $12.99, 10 postcards
for $8.99" />
...
```

1 To float every other image to the right, we first need to divide the images into two classes: the odd ones and the even ones.

```
...
img.odd {float:left;padding-right:10px}
img.even {float:right;padding-left:10px}
...
```

2 Next, we make the existing img style rule apply only to the img elements whose class is odd.

3 Finally, we add a second style rule to float the even images to the right (with padding on the left).

The first image continues to float to the left as before.

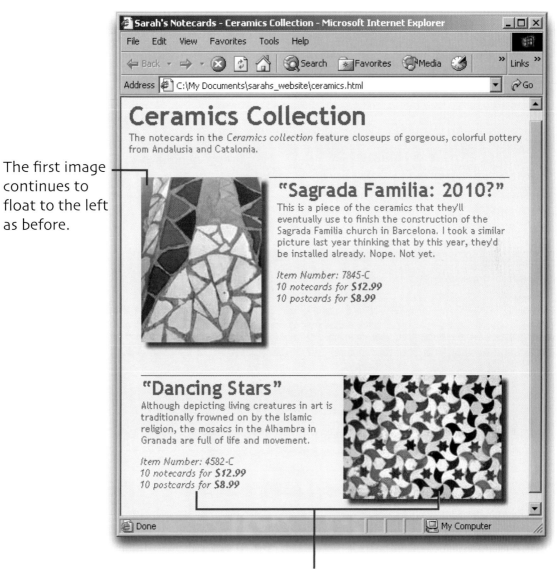

Ceramics Collection

The notecards in the *Ceramics collection* feature closeups of gorgeous, colorful pottery from Andalusia and Catalonia.

"Sagrada Familia: 2010?"

This is a piece of the ceramics that they'll eventually use to finish the construction of the Sagrada Familia church in Barcelona. I took a similar picture last year thinking that by this year, they'd be installed already. Nope. Not yet.

Item Number: 7845-C
10 notecards for $12.99
10 postcards for $8.99

"Dancing Stars"

Although depicting living creatures in art is traditionally frowned on by the Islamic religion, the mosaics in the Alhambra in Granada are full of life and movement.

Item Number: 4582-C
10 notecards for $12.99
10 postcards for $8.99

The even image "island" now floats to the right while its "water" flows to the left. We needed to put the padding on the left to separate the image from the descriptive text.

mimic shadow

```
. . .
img.odd {float:left;padding-right:10px}
img.even {float:right;padding-left:10px;
        background:#EDF2FF}
. . .
```

We'll change the even images' background color to the same light blue as the body's background.

The drop shadow makes it look as if there is a space between the first image and the blue line even though they're right next to one another.

The color of the padding comes from an element's background—which by default is transparent. By setting the image's background—and thus its padding—to the same light blue as the body's background, we cover up 10 pixels of the blue line and create the same effect that the shadow creates in the upper image.

finish inner page

Finish the inner page
by adding the necessary
HTML code to create
the last two postcard
divisions. (You can find
the example files online, if
you prefer. See page xiii.)

extra bits

save as html p. 6

- In fact, in this book, you'll be writing XHTML, which is the most current, most standard version of HTML. The extension is still .html.

- Don't choose the Save as Web Page command in Microsoft Word. It is designed for converting a Word document into HTML, not for saving a document already written in HTML.

- Once you save a document with the .html extension, double-clicking it will often open your browser, not the text editor. In order to edit the page, either open it from inside your text editor (using File > Open) or right-click it on the desktop, and choose Open with [your text editor].

start the web page p. 7

- Officially, web pages should begin with a DOCTYPE declaration, which describes the version of HTML being used. For example:

  <!DOCTYPE html PUBLIC "-//W3C//DTD XHTML 1.0 Transitional//EN"

  "http://www.w3.org/TR/xhtml1/DTD/xhtml1-transitional.dtd">

  <html xmlns="http://www.w3.org/1999/xhtml">

  But it's not the end of the world if you just start with <html>.

write a title p. 9

- The title of your web page is one of the key factors in getting it ranked on a search engine like Google. Use specific words in your title that reflect the content of your page.

color the background p. 13

- An element's background is transparent by default. That means that if it is on top of another element, you'll see the other element's background shining through.

- The part of a style rule that describes the elements that will be affected by the rule is called the selector. It can be as simple as an element's name as in the example here (body), or it can be more complex in order to select only certain elements that satisfy given criteria. We'll see some more complicated selectors in Chapter 2.

creating the inner pages

choose fonts p. 15

- The following fonts come with the standard installation of Internet Explorer for Windows and are thus likely to be installed on your visitor's computer: Andale Mono, Arial Black, Comic Sans MS, Georgia, Impact, Trebuchet MS, Verdana and Webdings. For more information, see http://www. microsoft.com/typography/fonts/ default.aspx.

- There is a font property which acts as a shortcut for specifying not only the font-family, but also the font-size, line-height, font-weight, font-style, and font-variant. For details, see Appendix B, CSS Reference.

- An element that is inside another element is called a child element. The outer element is called a parent element.

adjust spacing p. 18

- The margin is the amount of space around the outer edge of an element, beyond the padding and the border (which are discussed on pages 32 and 34, respectively). It is colorless.

- If you use one value, as in margin:0, it is applied to all four sides equally.

- If you use two values, as in margin: 5px 0, the first is used for the top and bottom and the second is used for the right and left.

- With three values, as in margin: 10px 5px 4px, the first is used for the top, the second for the right and left and the third for the bottom.

- If you use four values, as in margin: 10px 2px 5px 8px, they are applied to the top, right, bottom, and left, in clockwise order.

- You can add the margin to one particular side of the element by using margin-top, margin-bottom, margin-right, or margin-left instead of just margin. In that case, of course, just one value is required.

create a web image p. 19

- The techniques described on pages 19–23 are designed to be illustrative, not exhaustive—since there are many different image editors on the market. The most important thing to learn is that photos almost always need to be cropped or resized, adjusted, and compressed. You may need to consult your image editor's manual or help screens to figure out the exact steps it requires.

extra bits

format photos as jpeg p. 23

- When an image is compressed with JPEG, some details are permanently discarded. You should therefore only save an image as JPEG once, when you are finished making any other necessary adjustments. Repeatedly saving an image in JPEG format can make it blurry.

- For computer-generated images, use GIF format (with LZW compression). We'll discuss this more on page 67.

add photos to page p. 25

- You can create a folder within your web folder to organize your images, say sarahs_images. Then, the src attribute will need to reflect that new location: /sarahs_images/park_guell.jpg.

- While you can use the height and width attributes to change the size of the image in your web page, it's not the best method for doing so. To make an image smaller, crop (page 20) or resize it (page 22). To make an image bigger, reshoot it!

label a photo p. 26

- Insert non-breaking spaces ( ) between words in a label to avoid nasty line breaks like the one shown on page 26.

- The only limit I've found to the quantity of text you can put in a title is the amount of time your visitors have to read it before it automatically disappears.

- If your label contains double quotes, you can use single quotes to enclose the whole label. For example, title = 'These are the "Sagrada Familia" ceramics'.

use special characters p. 28

- You only need to use a character reference for a special symbol if that symbol is not part of your web page's encoding, which reflects the page's principal language. For web pages written in English on English operating systems, that means any symbols beyond the first 128 in ASCII. You'll find a list of these symbols with their corresponding character references in Appendix D.

- For full details about writing pages with large portions in other languages, see Chapter 20, "Symbols and Non-English Characters", in my HTML VQS (described on page xvi).

change font size p. 30

- You can set a specific font size in pixels (px), points (pt), centimeters (cm), millimeters (mm), or picas (pc). Only pixels should be used for setting a specific size on screen; the others are good for controlling printed output.

- You can also use keywords to specify a specific size—xx-small, x-small, small, medium, large, x-large, or xx-large—however, browsers interpret these keywords in different ways.

- You can set the font size relative to the parent element (that is, the element that contains the one you're defining) by using ems (em) or a percentage (%). You can also use the relative keywords larger or smaller.

- The line height can be specified as an absolute value in pixels (px), or relative to the element's font-size, either as a number (say, 1.2), as a percentage (120%), or in ems (em). The difference lies in how the values are inherited by elements contained in the one you're defining. We'll discuss this in more detail in Chapter 2.

pad the images p. 32

- The padding is the space between an element's content and its border (which is discussed on page 34).

- The padding is applied with the same system as the margin. See adjust spacing on page 49.

- Padding is the same color as the element's background.

- If two adjacent elements both have padding, both values are added together and may result in too much space. (In contrast, adjacent vertical margins are combined, resulting in a value equal to the larger of the two.)

draw a border p. 34

- The border is the outer edge of the padding and the inner edge of the margin.

- The border-style can be none, dotted, dashed, solid, double, groove, ridge, inset, or outset.

- The default border-style is none, which means if you don't specify a style, you won't get a border.

- You can apply only one aspect of a border (to one or more sides of an element) by using border-color, border-width, or border-style. Use one to four values in the same way as described for margins on page 49.

- You can apply one or more border aspects to one particular side of a border by using border-right, border-top, etc., along with up to three desired values.

extra bits

draw a border (cont.)

- You can even apply a single border aspect to a single side of an element with something like border-top-color.

- If you specify only some aspects of a border, the other aspects are set to their defaults.

add line breaks p. 37

- Note that the br element is empty. The text, 10 notecards for $12.99, is in the p element, not the br element.

add local formatting p. 38

- You can also use the logical HTML elements, strong and em (for emphasis) to add local formatting. Text marked with strong is usually displayed bold, em text is usually displayed in italics.

- You can make text bigger and smaller with big and small.

- You can format text as a subscript (sub) or superscript (sup).

- You can underline text with ins (for insert), and you can strike out text with del (for delete).

- Local formatting should only be used for small amounts of text. Use styles for whole paragraphs or divisions.

add structure p. 39

- The div element has no default formatting. However, it is a block-level element, which means it will always start on its own line.

clear floats p. 41

- The clear property can be set to both, left, right, or none.

2. creating the home page

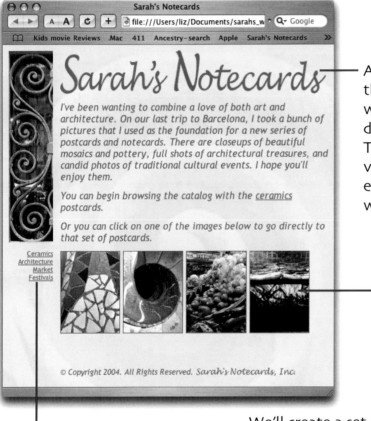

A home page is not only the front door to your web site but also the directory of its contents. The idea is to capture your visitors' interest as you explain who you are and why this site exists.

We'll create a set of images that function as links to the rest of the site, and then duplicate the links in the left-hand navigation bar in case for some reason the images should fail to load.

what we'll do

1 On pages 55–60, to get set up, we'll create and begin writing a new HTML file (index.html), apply to it the existing styles (sarahs_styles.css), create a new style sheet (home.css), and apply that too.

2 Next, from pages 61–64, we'll create a low-contrast background image and add it to the HTML code.

3 On pages 65–68 we'll create a GIF image for the header logo and add it to the HTML.

7 Last but not least, on pages 82–89, we'll create a left navigation bar with an image and four text links (to the same pages as the image links, just in case the images don't load).

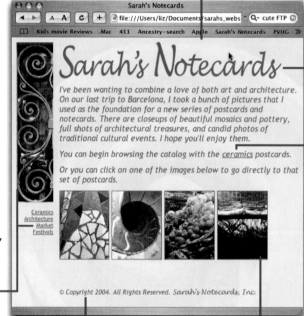

4 Next, on pages 69–72, we'll add the main paragraph and create a link to the ceramics.html page we created in Chapter 1. Then we'll make the link beautiful.

6 On pages 79–81, we'll add a copyright notice on the bottom of the page, complete with copyright symbol, and add some local styles.

5 On pages 73–78, we'll then create the four images that we'll use to link to the inner pages of our web site, add them to the HTML, and make them into links.

create a new html file

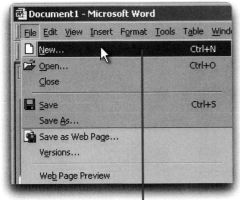

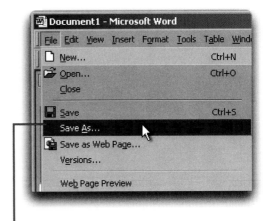

1 Choose File > New from your preferred text editor.

2 Before you start writing your web file, save it in the proper format by choosing File > Save As from your text editor or word processor (not Save as Web Page).

3 Be sure to save it in the proper folder (the same sarahs_website folder that we created on page 4).

4 Use index.html for the file name of the web page.

5 And, especially in Microsoft Word, be sure to save it in Plain Text or Text Only format (not HTML or Web page!).

start the home page

Always start your web page with
\<html\> (or !DOCTYPE, see page 48).

Next, comes the head
section.

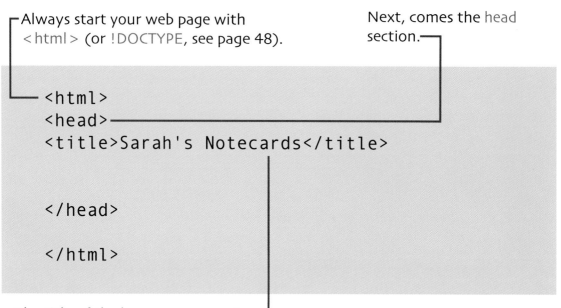

```
<html>
<head>
<title>Sarah's Notecards</title>


</head>

</html>
```

The title of the home page goes in
the head section between opening
and closing title tags.

The title is displayed in the browser's window bar,
often next to the browser's name.

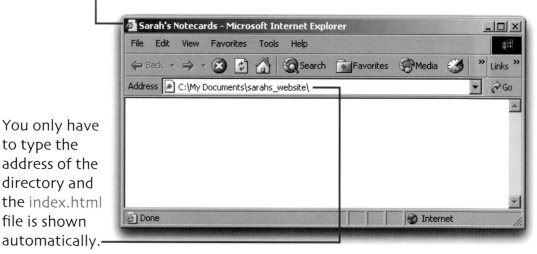

You only have
to type the
address of the
directory and
the index.html
file is shown
automatically.

creating the home page

structure the page

A web page's content is always enclosed in its body. The body on this page is further organized into two main divisions: a central content area (main) and a navigation bar (nav_bar).

```
   . . .
  </head>
  <body>
  <div class="main">



  </div>

  <div class="nav_bar">



  </div>
  </body>
  </html>
```

It's generally a good idea to name your divisions according to their purpose, not their appearance. Don't use spaces or punctuation, except the underscore (_).

creating the home page

link existing style sheet

```
. . .
<title>Sarah's Notecards</title>
<link rel="stylesheet" type="text/css"
href="sarahs_styles.css" />
. . .
```

Here we link our new index.html file to the style sheet that we created throughout Chapter 1, sarahs_styles.css. This makes it easy to use the same styles throughout your entire web site.

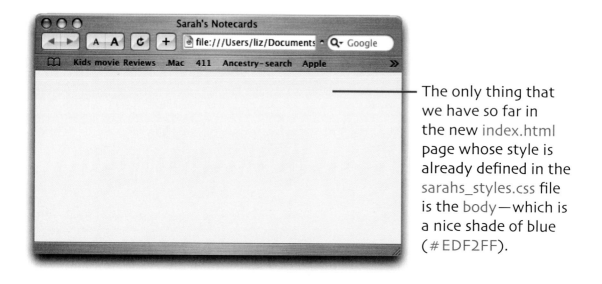

The only thing that we have so far in the new index.html page whose style is already defined in the sarahs_styles.css file is the body—which is a nice shade of blue (#EDF2FF).

creating the home page

create new style sheet

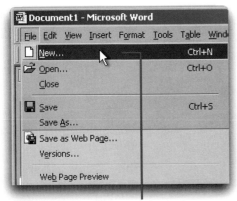

1 Choose File > New from your preferred text editor.

2 Before you start writing your style sheet, save it in the proper format by choosing File > Save As from your text editor or word processor.

3 Be sure to save it in the proper folder (the same sarahs_website folder that we created on page 4).

4 Use home.css for the name of the style sheet.

5 And be sure to save it in Plain Text or Text Only format.

link to new styles

The order in which style sheets are linked is very important. Style sheets that are linked later—like home.css here—take precedence over earlier style sheets—like sarahs_styles.css here. (We'll see this better as the chapter progresses.)

```
<head>
<title>Sarah's Notecards</title>
<link rel="stylesheet" type="text/css"
href="sarahs_styles.css" />
<link rel="stylesheet" type="text/css"
href="home.css" />
</head>

. . .
```

Type the new style sheet's file name exactly as you saved it on the previous page.

creating the home page

create a background

Here is the original image that I used to create the background. It has too much contrast to be a suitable background. In order for your visitors to read the content on your page, we'll have to reduce the contrast.

The image still has too much contrast.

Increase the brightness and reduce the contrast until the image detail all but disappears. (In Photoshop Elements, choose Enhance > Adjust Brightness/Contrast > Brightness/Contrast.)

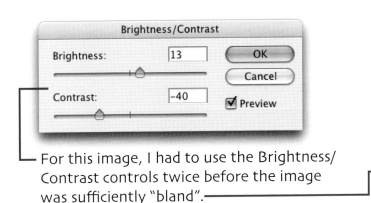

For this image, I had to use the Brightness/Contrast controls twice before the image was sufficiently "bland".

colorize background

You can then colorize the grayish, low-contrast image by changing the Hue/Saturation (Command-U in Photoshop Elements).

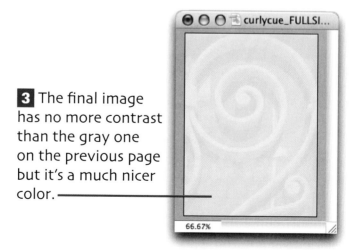

1 First, click the Colorize and Preview boxes.

2 Then experiment with the controls, being careful not to add more contrast, until you get the color you want.

3 The final image has no more contrast than the gray one on the previous page but it's a much nicer color.

creating the home page

save the background

We'll increase the size of the background image to 700 pixels wide so that it won't repeat unnecessarily. Since it's going to be in the background, the minor resulting blurriness won't be a problem.

Save For Web

Save an image to include in a Web page.
Save photographs as JPEG and images with limited colors as GIF.
The image preview shows how your image will look using the current settings.

OK
Cancel
Help

Settings: Custom

JPEG | Optimized
High | Quality: 60
Progressive
ICC Profile | Matte:

Image Size
Original Size
Width: 256 pixels
Height: 341 pixels

New Size
Width: 700 pixels
Height: 932 pixels
Percent: 273.44
Constrain Proportions
Apply

Original: "curlycue_FULLSIZE_original.jpg"
1.87M

JPEG
15.89K
4 sec @ 56.6Kbps

60 quality

Zoom: 100%

Preview in:

Animation
Loop
Frame Delay: 0.2

1 of 1

In fact, the blurring that results from increasing the image's size makes it a prime candidate for JPEG compression. Even at the relatively high quality level of 60, the image is squeezed down to little more than 15K. Call the image curly.jpg and place it in the sarahs_website folder.

add background image

This will be the first line of the home.css document that we created on page 59.

```
body {background: url(curly.jpg)}
```

Type the name of your background image exactly as you saved it on the previous page. As long as it's contained in the same folder as your style sheet, you don't need any additional path information.

The new background property conflicts with the background property that we set for body in the sarahs_styles.css file (where we said it should be EDF2FF blue). Since we linked this home.css file later (see page 60), it wins the fight and we get the curly.jpg image shown. However, if the image cannot be loaded for some reason, we'll get the EDF2FF blue background instead.

begin the header logo

In your image editor, start with a file around 600 pixels wide (at 72dpi)—about the same width as the average browser window—so you can judge visually how big your header should be.

If your program allows it, begin with a transparent background.

Because we will save the file as an image, you can take advantage of your font library to make a pleasing logo. This font is Lucida Handwriting.

make logo transparent

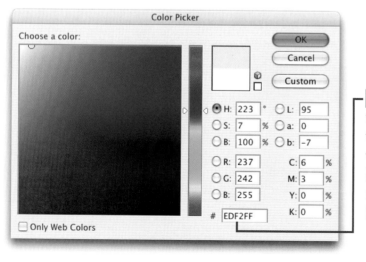

1 In Photoshop Elements, to make the header blend into the background, click Transparency in the Save For Web dialog box.

2 Then click Other in the Matte pop-up menu to make the Color Picker appear.

3 In the Color Picker, type EDF2FF to specify the color that the header will blend into. (Here we have it blend into the main color of our page's background.)

save logo as gif

1 Choose GIF format for computer-generated images like text and logos. (This is Photoshop Elements' Save For Web dialog box.)

2 Then click OK to save the image.

3 Call the file header_logo.gif and place it in the sarahs_website folder.

add header logo

```
. . .
<body>
<div class="main">
<p><img src="header_logo.gif" alt="Sarah's
Notecards" width="445" height="77" /></p>
. . .
```

The width of the header logo is just about perfect—slightly more narrow than the average web page.

Whenever you replace text with an image, you should reproduce the text in the alt attribute. This "translates" your GIF image for search engines like Google that can then use the information to set their rankings, or for software that makes web pages accessible, say to the blind.

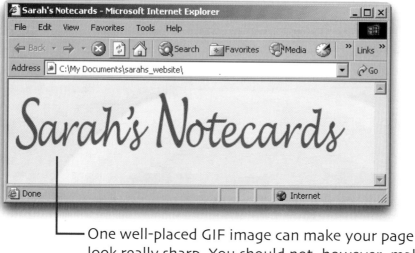

One well-placed GIF image can make your page look really sharp. You should not, however, make all your text into GIF images; GIFs are too hard to update, search, and rank, too inflexible, and not universal enough for the web.

creating the home page

add text

```
. . .
<p><img src="header_logo.gif" alt="Sarah's
Notecards" width="445" height="77" /></p>
<p>I've been wanting to combine a love of
both art and architecture. On our last trip
to Barcelona, I took a bunch of pictures that
I used as the foundation for a new series of
postcards and notecards. There are closeups
of beautiful mosaics and pottery, full shots
of architectural treasures, and candid photos
of traditional cultural events. I hope you'll
enjoy them. </p>
. . .
```

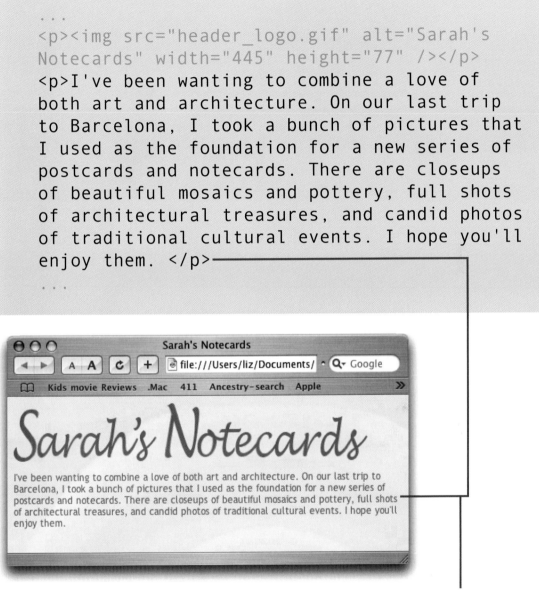

Our new paragraph gets its formatting from the styles in the sarahs_styles.css file that we created in Chapter 1. I think the text is too small for a home page introduction.

increase font size

```
p {font-size: 16px}
```

We'll increase the font size of the p elements on
the home page. Note that the p elements on the
inner pages will not be affected.

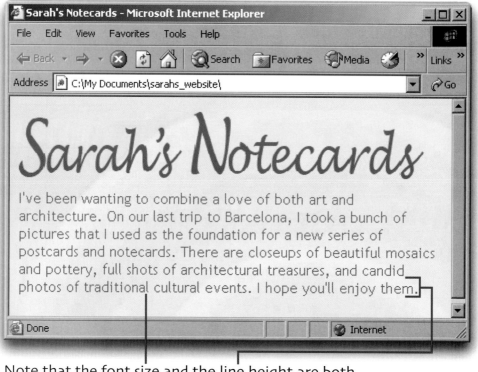

Note that the font size and the line height are both
increased. The p elements inherited a factor of 1.2 for the
line height from sarahs_styles.css, which gives a pleasing
value of 19.2 here (the new font size of 16 pixels times 1.2).

create a link

The anchor element (abbreviated as a) lets you create links to other pages, either on your site or on someone else's.

```
. . .
I hope you'll enjoy them.</p>

<p>You can begin browsing the catalog with
the <a href="ceramics.html">ceramics</a>
postcards.</p>

. . .
```

If the linked page is in the same directory as the page you're linking from, you don't need any additional path information besides the file name itself.

The text between the opening and closing a tags will be highlighted on your page and will "invite" your visitor's clicks.

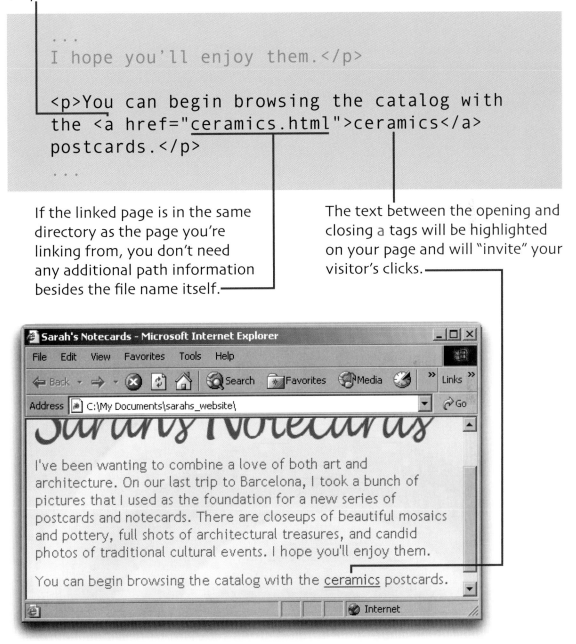

Sarah's Notecards - Microsoft Internet Explorer

File   Edit   View   Favorites   Tools   Help

Back   ·   ·   ·   Search   Favorites   Media   »   Links   »

Address   C:\My Documents\sarahs_website\   Go

Sarah's Notecards

I've been wanting to combine a love of both art and architecture. On our last trip to Barcelona, I took a bunch of pictures that I used as the foundation for a new series of postcards and notecards. There are closeups of beautiful mosaics and pottery, full shots of architectural treasures, and candid photos of traditional cultural events. I hope you'll enjoy them.

You can begin browsing the catalog with the ceramics postcards.

Internet

style the links

Instead of that familiar bright blue, we want both new (a:link) and already visited (a:visited) links to be the same color blue as our text (#4D65A0).

Remember that we can apply the same style rule to one or more kinds of elements by separating them with a comma (see page 33).

```
. . .
a:link, a:visited {color:#4D65A0}
a:focus, a:hover, a:active {color:#7A4DA0;
    text-decoration:none; font-weight:bold}
```

For links that are selected, say, by the Tab key (a:focus), are being pointed at (a:hover), or are being clicked (a:active), we want to apply a purple color (#7A4DA0), remove the underlining (text-decoration:none), and make them bold (font-weight:bold).

postcards and notecards. There are
nd pottery, full shots of architectural
traditional cultural events. I hope you'll

alog with the ceramics postcards.

Browsers underline links by default. Changing the color makes them a bit more subtle, without hiding them completely.

postcards and notecards. There are
nd pottery, full shots of architectural
traditional cultural events. I hope you'll

alog with the ceramics postcards.

ecards/ceramics.html"

When the visitor selects or points at the link (and, indeed, as they click it), the link calls attention to itself by losing its underline, and becoming bold and purple.

creating the home page

create little images

Part of our web page consists of four images that will serve as links to the inner pages of the site. They have to be little. One way to do this in Photoshop is to use the crop tool, and specify the desired final size in pixels (with a resolution of 72 dpi).

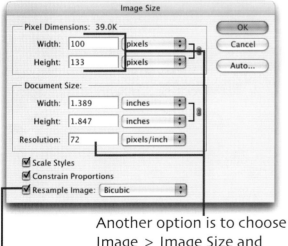

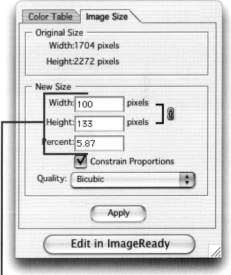

Another option is to choose Image > Image Size and specify the new size there in pixels (at 72 dpi).

The Resample Image box will have to be checked.

Or you can use the Image Size tab in the Save For Web dialog box.

create an images folder

Now that we've added the four little images to the sarahs_website folder, its contents are becoming a bit unorganized. (You can download the images from the web site—see page xiii.)

Choose File > New > Folder to create a new folder for the little images. Call it little.

Drag the four little images to the little folder.

make image links

There are two new paragraphs. The first introduces the image links, the other contains them.

The anchor (a) elements are virtually identical to the one on page 71. The difference is that instead of enclosing text, they enclose an image.

```
. . .
the <a href="ceramics.html">ceramics</a>
postcards.</p>
<p>Or you can click on one of the images below
to go directly to that set of postcards.</p>

<p><a href="ceramics.html">
<img src="little/sagrada_lit.jpg" width="100"
height="133" alt="Ceramics" /></a>
<a href="architecture.html">
<img src="little/spiral_lit.jpg" width="100"
height="133" alt="Architecture" /></a>
<a href="market.html">
<img src="little/market_lit.jpg" width="100"
height="133" alt="Market" /></a>
<a href="festivals.html">
<img src="little/festival_lit.jpg" width="100"
height="133" alt="Festivals" /></a>
</p>
. . .
```

Each img element begins after its respective opening < a > tag and ends before the corresponding closing </a> tag.

Since the images are in the little folder, you must precede the file name with the folder name (little) and a slash (/).

make image links (continued)

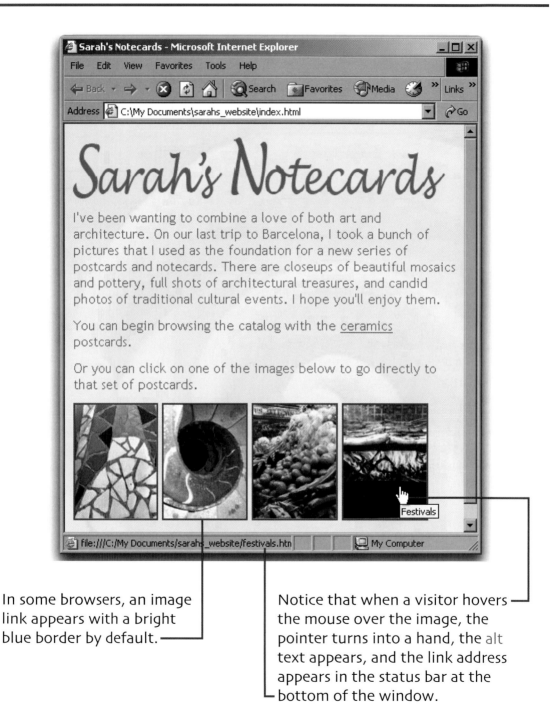

In some browsers, an image link appears with a bright blue border by default.

Notice that when a visitor hovers the mouse over the image, the pointer turns into a hand, the alt text appears, and the link address appears in the status bar at the bottom of the window.

creating the home page

adjust link borders

```
. . .
<p><a href="ceramics.html">
<img src="little/sagrada_lit.jpg" width="100"
height="133" alt="Ceramics" class="little"/>
</a>
. . .
```

Add a class attribute, set to little, to each of the four image links.

```
. . .
img.little {border: 1px solid #4D65A0}
```

Then we'll create a style rule that will add a 1 pixel rule just around those images in links—but with our blue (#4D65A0), not the default bright blue that browsers use for links.

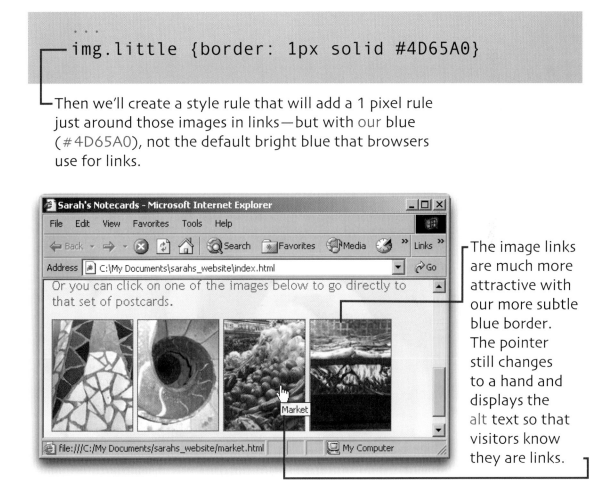

The image links are much more attractive with our more subtle blue border. The pointer still changes to a hand and displays the alt text so that visitors know they are links.

keep images together

Add a class attribute set to image_links to the p element that contains the image links.

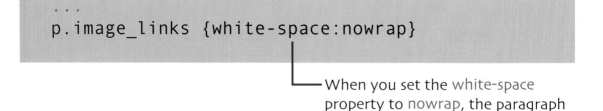

```
. . .
<p class="image_links"><a href="ceramics.html">
. . .
```

```
. . .
p.image_links {white-space:nowrap}
```

When you set the white-space property to nowrap, the paragraph is displayed with no line breaks.

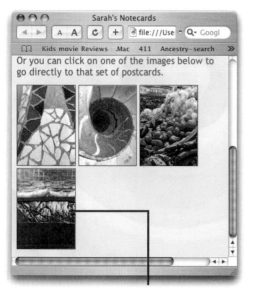

Before: If your visitor makes the window too narrow, the images wrap to the next line. The effect is not pretty.

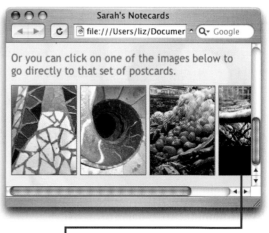

After: No matter how narrow the window, the image links will stay together on the same line.

creating the home page

add the copyright

Add a new paragraph to contain the copyright information. We'll add the copyright class so that we can format it later.

Use © to add the copyright symbol (©). You can find a whole list of references for symbols in Appendix D.

```
. . .
<img src="little/festival_lit.jpg"
alt="Festivals" width="100" height="133"
class="little" /></a></p>

<p class="copyright">&copy; Copyright 2004.
All Rights Reserved. Sarah's Notecards, Inc.
</p>

</div>
. . .
```

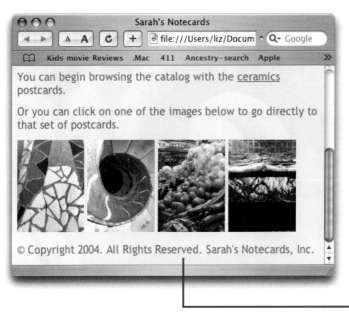

The copyright information begins with the basic styles that are already applied to all p elements (some of which are inherited from the body element).

make copyright smaller

```
. . .
p.image_links {white-space:nowrap}

p.copyright {font-size: smaller;
             padding-top: 40px}
```

The smaller value for the font-size property is calculated with respect to the element that contains this element (called the parent element), which in this case is the main div.

We'll also add padding to the top of the copyright paragraph to keep it a respectable distance from the rest of the content.

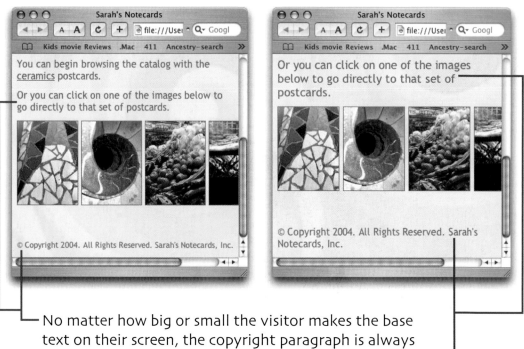

No matter how big or small the visitor makes the base text on their screen, the copyright paragraph is always one size smaller than the rest of the text in the div.

add styles in html

The span element has no default formatting and so works well for adding styles to a chunk of text that is otherwise hard to identify.

The style attribute is followed by an equals sign (=) and then a double quotation mark ("). Then add the CSS properties in the same property:value format as you've been doing all through this book.

```
...
<p class="copyright">&copy; Copyright 2004.
All Rights Reserved.<span style="font-family:
'Lucida Handwriting'">Sarah's Notecards,
Inc.</span>
</p>

</div>
...
```

Values that need to be enclosed in quotes should use single quotes (') instead of double ones ("), so they are not confused with the double quotes that delimit the value of the style attribute.

© Copyright 2004. All Rights Reserved. *Sarah's Notecards, Inc.*

The font will only display correctly if it is available on the visitor's system (as shown here). Otherwise, it will be ignored.

create a navigation bar

A navigation bar is a common device for helping your visitors find all the pages on your site. Ours runs along the left side of the page and consists of a long image followed by four text links.

You can download the image from the web site. It's called leftcurls.jpg and is the same image that the background came from originally.

The links go to the same pages as the image links we just created. If the images should not load properly for some reason, these links will give our visitors another way to get to the inner pages of our site.

begin navigation bar

```
. . .
Handwriting'"> Sarah's Notecards, Inc.</a></p>
</div>

<div class="nav_bar">
<p><img src="leftcurls.jpg" alt="" width="75"
height="314" /></p>
. . .
```

It's a good idea to start a navigation bar division after the main content. That way, if the styles don't work for some reason, the content will still be the first thing your visitors see.

Our navigation bar starts with the long image. Since it's just used for decoration, no alt text is necessary.

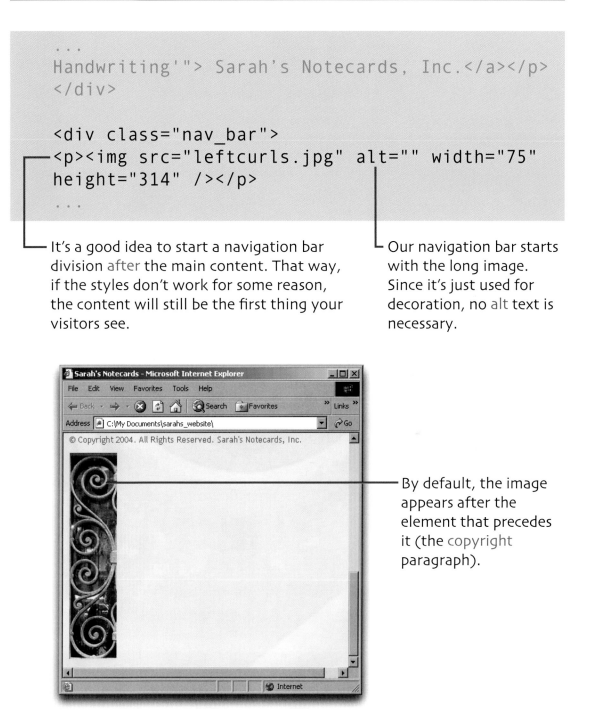

By default, the image appears after the element that precedes it (the copyright paragraph).

position navigation bar

```
   . . .
div.nav_bar {position: absolute;
             left: 10px;
             top: 10px}
```

The position property determines if a given element
should be part of the flow (that is, naturally appear
after the element that precedes it), or be positioned
absolutely as here, and thus be removed from the
flow and begin 10 pixels from the left (left: 10px)
and 10 pixels to the top (top: 10px) of the parent
element, which is the body, in this case.

The nav_bar div has
been removed from
the flow and, instead
of appearing after the
copyright paragraph, it
appears 10 pixels from
the left and 10 pixels
from the top of the body
element, its parent.
We'll fix that overlap on
the next page.

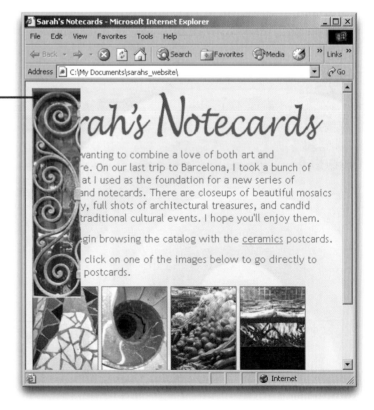

move main div over

```
    . . .
div.nav_bar {position: absolute;
            left: 10px;
            top: 10px}
div.main {margin-left:90px}
```

We'll add a left margin of 90 pixels to the entire main div to leave room for the 75 pixel-wide navigation bar image.

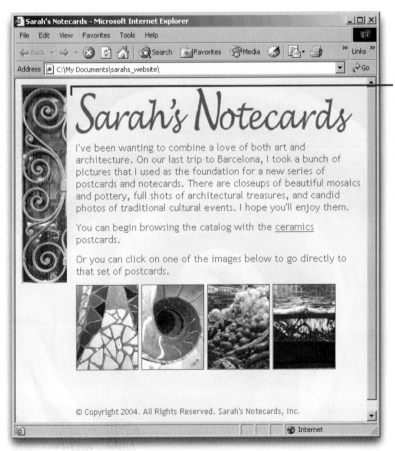

The contents of the two div elements now sit side by side. The extra 15 pixels (90 from the margin minus 75 from the image width) leave a pleasing gap between the two div elements.

add links to nav-bar

```
. . .
<div class="nav_bar">
<img src="leftcurls.jpg" alt="" width="75"
height="314" />
<p><a href="ceramics.html">Ceramics</a>
<br /><a href="architecture.html">
Architecture</a>
<br /><a href="market.html">Market</a>
<br /><a href="festivals.html">Festivals</a>
<br /></p>
. . .
```

Here we recreate the four image links—both to reinforce the navigation system in general, as well as to offer an alternative should the images not load for some reason.

The links get their formatting from the styles we defined earlier (on page 72). They're too big; we'll fix them on the next few pages.

creating the home page

align links to right

```
. . .
div.nav_bar {position: absolute; left: 10px;
top: 10px; text-align: right}
div.main {margin-left:90px}
```

The links will look better in the navigation bar if they're all aligned to the right (text-align:right).

The links (and indeed, the leftcurls.jpg file) are aligned to the right edge of the nav_bar div. The width of that div is determined by the largest element it contains, which in this case is the set of links. They're so big that they're pushing the whole nav_bar div over onto the contents of the main div. We'll fix that on the next page.

reduce size of links

```
. . .
div.nav_bar {position: absolute; left: 10px;
top: 10px; text-align: right}
div.nav_bar a {font-size: 11px}
div.main {margin-left:90px}
```

The space says "only apply this style to the a elements that are in the nav_bar div".

When the links are reduced in size, the nav_bar div itself is reduced in size and no longer overlaps the text in the main div. The width of the navigation bar is still determined by the widest element it contains, but that is now the leftcurls.jpg image.

italicize main content

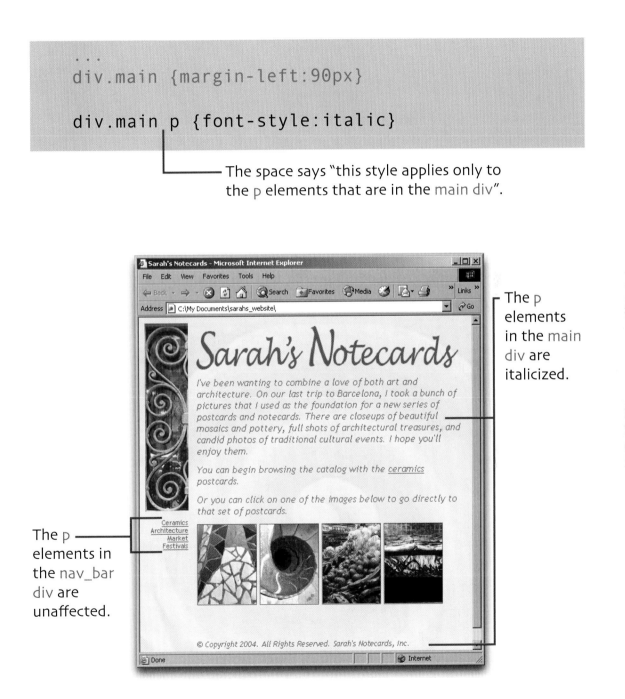

```
...
div.main {margin-left:90px}

div.main p {font-style:italic}
```

The space says "this style applies only to the p elements that are in the main div".

The p elements in the main div are italicized.

Sarah's Notecards

I've been wanting to combine a love of both art and architecture. On our last trip to Barcelona, I took a bunch of pictures that I used as the foundation for a new series of postcards and notecards. There are closeups of beautiful mosaics and pottery, full shots of architectural treasures, and candid photos of traditional cultural events. I hope you'll enjoy them.

You can begin browsing the catalog with the ceramics postcards.

Or you can click on one of the images below to go directly to that set of postcards.

Ceramics
Architecture
Market
Festivals

© Copyright 2004. All Rights Reserved. Sarah's Notecards, Inc.

The p elements in the nav_bar div are unaffected.

extra bits

create a new html file p. 55

- When you name a file index.html, it is designated as the default file that should open when someone types the address of the directory that contains it. For example, at my site, when someone types http://www.cookwood.com/ the file that they actually see is http://www.cookwood.com/index.html.

link existing style sheet p. 58

- The genius of style sheets is that you can use the same style sheet for as many pages as you want. Not only does this save you time in defining the styles for each page, but it makes global changes very easy to implement.

link to new styles p. 60

- You can link to as many style sheets from a single HTML page as you like. Style sheets that are linked later generally take precedence over conflicting rules from earlier style sheets—as long as the rules share the same level of specificity. So, if an earlier style sheet says p elements should be blue and a later one says they should be red, they will be red. If the earlier style sheet says p elements of class special should be purple, the later, but more general red rule will not affect those special p elements.

begin the header logo p. 65

- For this logo, I scaled the letters horizontally, used oversized capitals, and then reduced the space between the caps and the lowercase letters that follow them. You needn't go to such lengths, however. Simply choosing an attractive font is half of the battle.

add header logo p. 68

- The alt text can contain single straight quotes as long as it is enclosed in double quotes. If you want the alt text to contain double quotes, you must enclose it in single quotes (or use the character reference).

- Since the paragraphs in our main sarahs_styles.css style sheet have a bottom margin but no top margin (page 18), we'll enclose the GIF image in a paragraph. That way there will be a bit of space between the image and the paragraph below it (that we'll add next).

increase font size p. 70

- If we had used a percentage instead of a factor to set the line-height property for p elements in the sarahs_styles.css file, the line height would be inherited a different way. Instead of multiplying the percentage by a new font size, it would be the computed value (say, 120% of the original 12 pixels, or 14.4 pixels) that would be inherited, regardless of the new font size.

create a link p. 71

- You can create links to pages on other web sites by adding the full URL (including the http protocol part) in the href attribute. For example, to link to my site, use < a href = "http://www.cookwood. com" > go to Liz's site < /a > .

style the links p. 72

- Because a link can be in more than one state at a time, say, both unvisited and being pointed at, it's a good idea to style your links in order: link, visited, focus, hover, and then active.

- The text-decoration property can also accept values of underline, overline, line-through, blink, none, or inherit.

- The font-weight property can accept the following values: normal, bold, bolder, lighter, 100, 200, 300, 400, 500, 600, 700, 800, 900, or inherit.

create little images p. 73

- You can create these images yourself or get them from the web site: http://www.cookwood.com/ htmlvqj/

make image links p. 75

- You can link to nested folders by using additional folder names and slashes (/). So, if there were an image called mosaic.jpg in a folder called ceramics in the little folder you would link to it from a file that was in the sarahs_website folder by using little/ceramics/ mosaic.jpg.

- You can control the appearance of the cursor itself with the cursor property. You can consult my HTML VQS (see page xvi in the introduction) for more details.

extra bits

adjust link borders p. 77

- While some browsers show an empty image box when images don't load properly, others don't (below left). If the images have a CSS border, the border shows up even if the image doesn't and the visitor will more easily realize that there is a link there (below right).

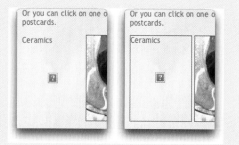

keep images together p. 78

- Use a value of pre for the white-space property to have the browser display all the returns and spaces in the original text. Use a value of normal to treat white space as usual.

make copyright smaller p. 80

- The font-size property also can be set to larger.

- You can also set the font-size property to a factor or to a percentage of the parent element's font size.

add styles in html p. 81

- The styles that you add with the style attribute within an HTML element take precedence over styles in a local or linked style sheet.

position navigation bar p. 84

- An element can also be positioned relative to its normal position in the flow (offset with the values of top and left), or it can be fixed to a static position on the window. However the latter property is only recently becoming more widely supported by browsers.

move main div over p. 85

- You may find it interesting to note that the div elements themselves are not side by side. Rather, the nav_bar div is on top of the main div. However, since the content of the main div has a left margin of 90 pixels, the illusion is that they're next to each other.

align links to right p. 87

- You can set the width manually in pixels or as a percentage of the parent element with the width property (e.g., width:100px). The relationship between the width, margin, border, and the padding properties is somewhat complex. See my HTML VQS for details.

3. publishing your web site

Once you've created your web site, the only step left is to make it available to the Internet by publishing it on a server and then letting people know it's there.

get a web host

Most ISPs (from whom you get your Internet connection) offer a small amount of free space—perhaps 25Mb—for a web site. Your address typically looks like the ISP's name, followed by a tilde (~) followed by your user name.

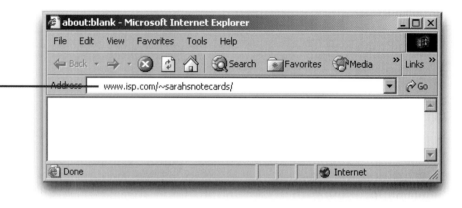

If you need more space or power, you can contract the services of a dedicated web host. Their job is to make your web files available to the Internet. They often offer not only additional space but the ability to run scripts, use databases, employ shopping carts, and more. You can research web hosts at webhostingratings.com.

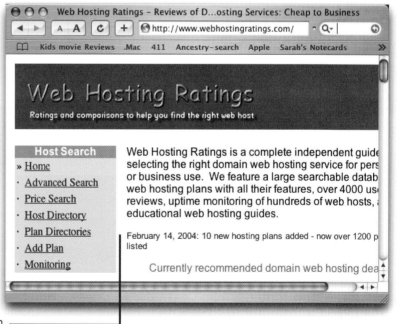

publishing your web site

get a web domain

Whether you have your site hosted by your ISP or by a dedicated web host, you also have the option of registering your own domain name (search for domain registration on Google). Having your own domain name makes your site look much more professional—and it makes it easier to get to, since the address is presumably easier to remember. And if you become dissatisfied with your current web host, you can leave it behind and take your domain name (and current visitors) with you to a new host.

set up the ftp program

1 You use an FTP program to transfer files from your computer to the server. This one is Cute FTP for Windows, but any FTP program is fine (see extra bits). Open the Site Manager (or New Connection dialog box, as it's known in Fetch for Mac).

2 Give this group of settings a name—typically, that of your web site, but it doesn't really matter.

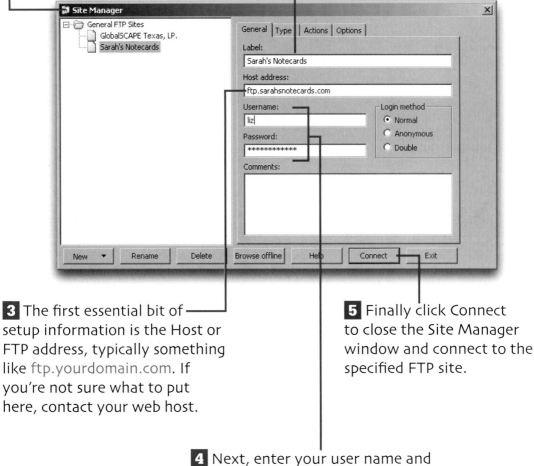

3 The first essential bit of setup information is the Host or FTP address, typically something like ftp.yourdomain.com. If you're not sure what to put here, contact your web host.

5 Finally click Connect to close the Site Manager window and connect to the specified FTP site.

4 Next, enter your user name and password. (Your web host should have provided you with these as well.)

publishing your web site

transfer files to server

1 Navigate through your computer's file system until you find the sarahs_website folder that you created throughout this book.

Cute FTP gives you the connection status in the window bar.

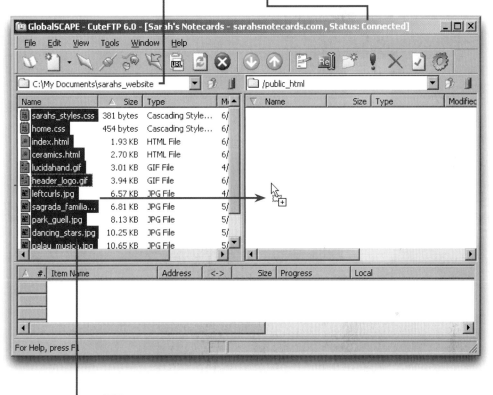

2 Select the files from the sarahs_website folder on your computer and drag them over to the FTP site.

test pages online

Once you've uploaded all your files, be sure to go online and test that your page is working properly. This page, for example, is missing a few images.

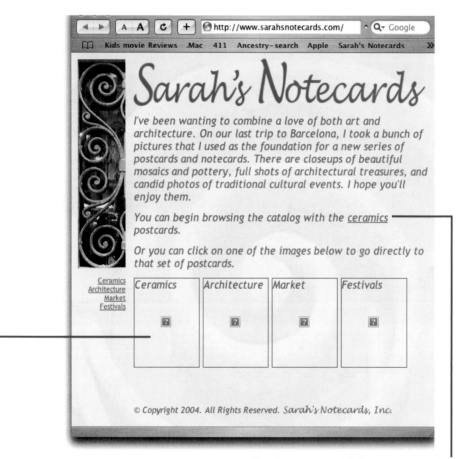

It's also a good idea to test all your links to make sure they lead where they should.

fix and retest

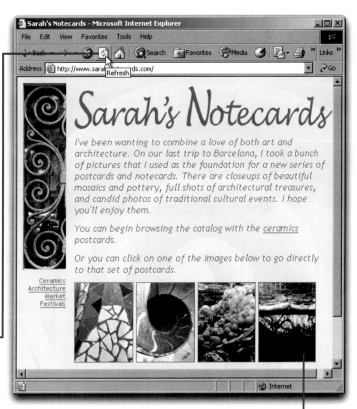

The error in this case was rather common, at least for me: I forgot to upload the little folder, together with the images it contains.

Once the problem has been fixed, choose View > Refresh from your browser. Or click the Refresh icon on the browser's toolbar.

The images now appear as they should.

get indexed

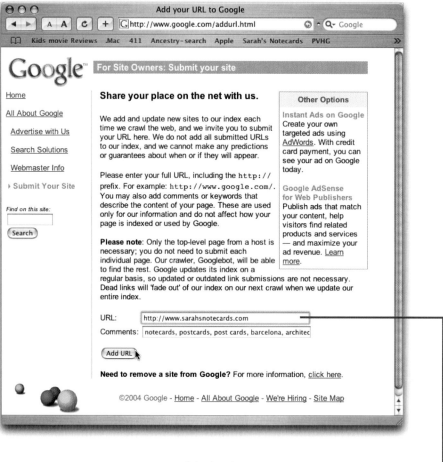

Once your site is published, you can invite Google to visit and add your site to its index by sending your URL (web address) through the Submit your site page at http://www.google.com/addurl.html.

extra bits

get a web host p. 94

- Questions that you should ask a prospective web host include how much they charge each month, how much they charge for "setup", if they have a money-back guarantee, if they have toll-free or email tech support, what their guaranteed uptime is (the percentage they are actually connected to the Internet serving your files), how much space you have on the server, and how many gigabytes you're allowed to serve each month (then divide this by the total size of all your web site files to determine how many users you'll be allowed to have).

get a web domain p. 95

- For a non-professional site, the most important reason to get your own domain name is so that you don't have to change your site's address (or your email) should you decide to change your web host (or ISP). I highly recommend it.

- There used to be only one company that could register domains: Network Solutions. That's no longer the case, and you can often get a better deal by going to the competition.

set up the ftp program p. 96

- Only your web host can tell you what the FTP address is for your site. If you get web space from your ISP, they often have this information on their web site.

- Your web host is also the only one who will know what your user name and password are (though it's often the same as what you use to get your email).

- Fetch for Macintosh is an excellent FTP program. Cute FTP also has a Macintosh version. And there's also WS_FTP for Windows, from Ipswitch.com, among many other possibilities.

transfer files to server p. 97

- As long as the files on the server have the same relative location with respect to the other files, all the links and images will continue to work. So, if index.html and ceramics.html were in the same sarahs_website folder on your computer, they should be in the same folder on your server. In the same way, since the link images were in the little folder on your computer, they should also be in a little folder on the server.

- Transferring files with other FTP programs is virtually the same as with Cute FTP. The basic process is setup, connect, and transfer.

transfer files to server (cont.)

- Some FTP programs require you to set the upload format. In that case use ASCII for text (HTML and CSS files) and Binary for images.

test pages online p. 98

- Missing images is one of the most common problems with a web page. (Remember that we duplicated the links to prepare for this eventuality.) The images may not have been uploaded, may not have been uploaded to the proper folder, or may not have been uploaded properly (images must be uploaded in binary format, and not all FTP programs do that automatically). Another common problem with images is that the file name in the src attribute of the img element does not exactly match the file name of the actual image, including upper and lowercase letters.

- It's also not a bad idea to test your web pages on a variety of browsers and platforms (Windows, Macintosh, Unix). While browsers have begun to embrace the standards that will make such testing unnecessary, there are still important differences, especially with older browsers in wide use (particularly Internet Explorer 5.5 for Windows).

- My number one tip for troubleshooting is to check the easy things first. I can't tell you how many times I've spent hours going over some new tricky technique just to find that the problem was that I misspelled the file name, or a too familiar attribute. Once you've ruled out the obvious culprits, then you can look for more complicated answers.

get indexed p. 100

- There are people who make a living by getting web sites indexed. There are three important techniques: 1. Use the words that people will search for in order to find you (called keywords) throughout your site and in a meaningful way, especially in the title, headers, and first paragraph. 2. Get linked from other sites. 3. Submit your site to Google.

appendix a:
html reference

In this appendix, you'll find a listing of the HTML elements and attributes that we've covered in this book. If you'd like to see what other HTML elements there are, you can consult my complete listing online: http://www.cookwood.com/html/ (in the extras section).

html reference

element/ attribute	description
— most tags —	The following attributes may be used with most HTML elements
class	For identifying a set of tags in order to apply styles (p. 35)
style	For adding local style sheet information (p. 81)
title	For labeling elements with tool tips (p. 26)
!DOCTYPE	Theoretically required. For indicating the version of HTML used (p. 48)
a	For creating links (p. 71)
href	For specifying the web address (URL) of the page that the link goes to
b	For displaying text in boldface (p. 38)
body	For enclosing the main content of a page (p. 10)
br	For creating a line break (p. 37)
div	For dividing a page into logical sections (p. 39, 57)
class	For giving a name to each class of divisions
h1, h2, ... h6	For creating headers (p. 14, 27)
head	For creating head section of a page (p. 8)
html	For identifying a text file as a web page (p. 7)
i	For displaying text in italics (p. 38)
img	For inserting images on a page (p. 25)
alt	For offering alternate text that is displayed if the image is not
src	For specifying the web address (URL) of the image
width, height	For specifying the size of the image so that the page is loaded more quickly
link	For linking to an external style sheet (p. 12, 58, 60)
href	For specifying the web address (URL) of the style sheet
type	For noting a style sheet's MIME type
rel	For indicating that the link is to a style sheet
p	For creating new paragraphs (p. 17)
span	For creating custom character styles (p. 81)
class	For naming individual custom character styles
title	Required. For creating the title of the page in the title bar area (p. 9)

appendix b:
css reference

In this appendix, you'll find an alphabetical listing of the CSS properties that we've covered in this book. You can find a complete listing of CSS properties on my web site: http://www.cookwood.com/html in the extras section.

css reference

property/values	description/notes
background any combination of the values for background-attachment, background-color, background-image, background-repeat, and/or background-position, or inherit	for changing the background color and image of elements (p. 13, 64) initial value depends on individual properties; not inherited; percentages allowed for background-position
background-color either a color, transparent, or inherit	for setting just the background color of an element (p. 13) initial value: transparent; not inherited
background-image either a URL, none, or inherit	for setting just the background image of an element (p. 64) initial value: none; not inherited
border any combination of the values of border-width, border-style, and/or a color, or inherit	for defining all aspects of a border on all sides of an element (p. 34) initial value depends on individual properties; not inherited
border-color from one to four colors, transparent, or inherit	for setting only the color of the border on one or more sides of an element (p. 34, 51) initial value: the element's color property; not inherited
border-style one to four of the following values: none, dotted, dashed, solid, double, groove, ridge, inset, outset, inherit	for setting only the style of a border on one or more sides of an element (p. 34, 51) initial value: none; not inherited
border-top, border-right, border-bottom, border-left any combination of a single value each for border-width, border-style, and/or a color, or use inherit.	for defining all three border properties at once on only one side of an element (p. 34, 51) initial value depends on individual values; not inherited
border-top-color, border-right-color, border-bottom-color, border-left-color one color or inherit	for defining just the border's color on only one side of an element (p. 34, 51) initial value: the value of the color property; not inherited
border-top-style, border-right-style, border-bottom-style, border-left-style one of none, dotted, dashed, solid, double, groove, ridge, inset, outset, or inherit	for defining just the border's style on only one side of an element (p. 34, 51–52) initial value: none; not inherited
border-top-width, border-right-width, border-bottom-width, border-left-width one of thin, medium, thick, or a length	for defining just the border's width on only one side of an element (p. 34, 51) initial value: medium; not inherited

property/values	description/notes
border-width one to four of the following values: thin, medium, thick, or a length	for defining the border's width on one or more sides of an element (p. 34, 51) initial value: medium; not inherited
clear one of none, left, right, both, or inherit	for keeping elements from floating on one or both sides of an element (p. 41) initial value: none; may only be applied to block-level elements; not inherited
color a color or inherit	for setting the foreground color of an element (p. 16) initial value: parent's color, some colors are set by browser; inherited
float one of left, right, none, inherit	for determining on which side of an element other elements are permitted to float (p. 31, 44) initial value: none; may not be applied to positioned elements or generated content; not inherited
font if desired, any combination of the values for font-style, font-variant, and font-weight followed by the required font-size, an optional value for line-height, and the also required font-family, or use inherit	for setting at least the font family and size, and optionally the style, variant, weight, and line-height of text initial value depends on individual properties; inherited; percentages allowed for values of font-size and line-height
font-family one or more quotation mark-enclosed font names followed by an optional generic font name, or use inherit	for choosing the font family for text (p. 15) initial value: depends on browser; inherited
font-size an absolute size, a relative size, a length, a percentage, or inherit	for setting the size of text (p. 30) initial value: medium; the computed value is inherited; percentages refer to parent element's font size
font-style either normal, italic, oblique, or inherit	for making text italic (p. 36, 89) initial value: normal; inherited
font-weight either normal, bold, bolder, lighter, 100, 200, 300, 400, 500, 600, 700, 800, 900, or inherit	for applying, removing, and adjusting bold formatting (p. 72) initial value: normal; the numeric values are considered keywords and not integers (you can't choose 150, for example); inherited

appendix b: css reference

css reference

property/values	description/notes
left either a length, percentage, auto, or inherit	for setting the distance that an element should be offset from its parent element's left edge (p. 84) initial value: auto; may only be applied to positioned elements; not inherited; percentages refer to width of containing block
line-height either normal, a number, a length, a percentage, or inherit	for setting the amount of space between lines of text (p. 30) initial value: normal; inherited; percentages refer to the font size of the element itself
margin one to four of the following: length, percentage, auto, or inherit	for setting the amount of space between one or more sides of an element's border and its parent element (p. 18) initial value depends on browser and on value of width; not inherited; percentages refer to width of containing block
margin-top, margin-right, margin-bottom, margin-left either a length, percentage, auto, or inherit	for setting the amount of space between only one side of an element's border and its parent element initial value: 0; not inherited; percentages refer to width of containing block; the values for margin-right and margin-left may be overridden if sum of width, margin-right, and margin-left are larger than parent element's containing block
padding one to four lengths or percentages, or inherit	for specifying the distance between one or more sides of an element's content area and its border (p. 40) initial value depends on browser: not inherited; percentages refer to width of containing block
padding-top, padding-right, padding-bottom, padding-left either a length, percentage, or inherit	for specifying the distance between one side of an element's content area and its border (p. 32, 44) initial value: 0; not inherited; percentages refer to width of containing block
position either static, relative, absolute, fixed, or inherit	for determining how an element should be positioned with respect to the document's flow (p. 84) initial value: static; may not be applied to generated content; not inherited
text-align one of left, right, center, justify, a string, or inherit	for aligning text (p. 87) initial value depends on browser and writing direction; may only be applied to block-level elements; inherited

property/values	description/notes
text-decoration any combination of underline, overline, line-through, and blink, or none or inherit	for decorating text (mostly with lines) (p. 72) initial value: none; not inherited
top either a length, percentage, auto, or inherit	for setting the distance that an element should be offset from its parent element's top edge (p. 84) initial value: auto; may only be applied to positioned elements; not inherited; percentages refer to height of containing block
white-space either normal, pre, nowrap, or inherit	for specifying how white space should be treated (p. 78) initial value: normal; may only be applied to block-level elements; inherited
width either a length, percentage, auto, or inherit	for setting the width of an element (p. 92) initial value: auto; may not be applied to non-replaced inline elements, table rows, or row groups; not inherited; percentages refer to width of containing block

appendix c: colors

Colors add life to your web site. In this appendix, you'll see how to create the color codes that you'll use in your style sheets. You'll also find a table of the sixteen named colors, as well as a selection of 234 colors, along with their corresponding codes, that you can use as is or as a foundation for choosing your own.

color codes

Here is a bit of one of the style sheets created with this book.

Begin the color code with the hash symbol (#).

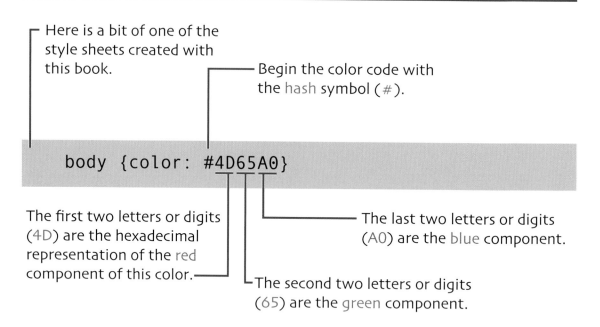

`body {color: #4D65A0}`

The first two letters or digits (4D) are the hexadecimal representation of the red component of this color.

The last two letters or digits (A0) are the blue component.

The second two letters or digits (65) are the green component.

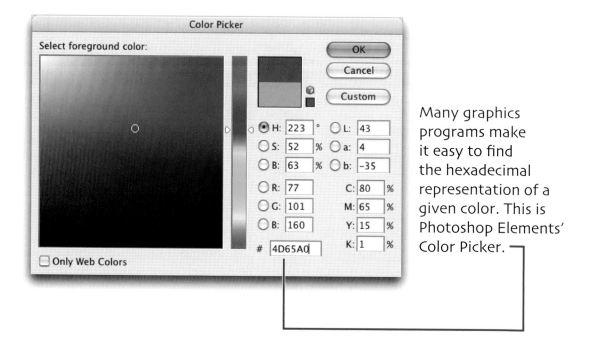

Many graphics programs make it easy to find the hexadecimal representation of a given color. This is Photoshop Elements' Color Picker.

sixteen named colors

There are sixteen
predefined colors.

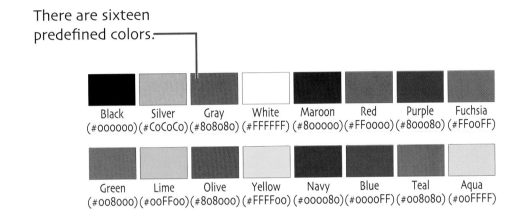

Black	Silver	Gray	White	Maroon	Red	Purple	Fuchsia
(#000000)	(#C0C0C0)	(#808080)	(#FFFFFF)	(#800000)	(#FF0000)	(#800080)	(#FF00FF)

Green	Lime	Olive	Yellow	Navy	Blue	Teal	Aqua
(#008000)	(#00FF00)	(#808000)	(#FFFF00)	(#000080)	(#0000FF)	(#008080)	(#00FFFF)

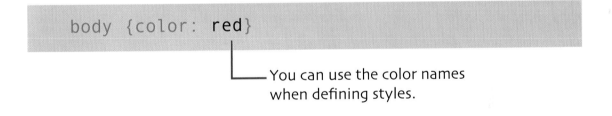

```
body {color: red}
```

You can use the color names
when defining styles.

a selection of colors

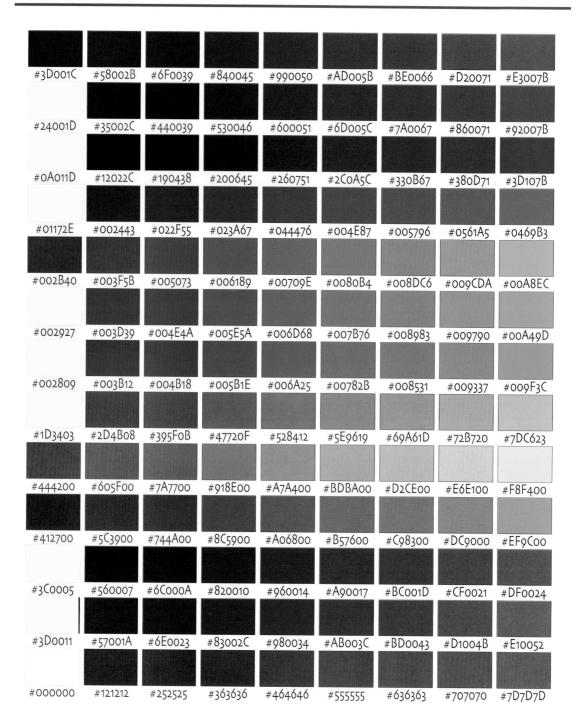

#3D001C	#58002B	#6F0039	#840045	#990050	#AD005B	#BE0066	#D20071	#E3007B
#24001D	#35002C	#440039	#530046	#600051	#6D005C	#7A0067	#860071	#92007B
#0A011D	#12022C	#190438	#200645	#260751	#2C0A5C	#330B67	#380D71	#3D107B
#01172E	#002443	#022F55	#023A67	#044476	#004E87	#005796	#0561A5	#0469B3
#002B40	#003F5B	#005073	#006189	#00709E	#0080B4	#008DC6	#009CDA	#00A8EC
#002927	#003D39	#004E4A	#005E5A	#006D68	#007B76	#008983	#009790	#00A49D
#002809	#003B12	#004B18	#005B1E	#006A25	#00782B	#008531	#009337	#009F3C
#1D3403	#2D4B08	#395F0B	#47720F	#528412	#5E9619	#69A61D	#72B720	#7DC623
#444200	#605F00	#7A7700	#918E00	#A7A400	#BDBA00	#D2CE00	#E6E100	#F8F400
#412700	#5C3900	#744A00	#8C5900	#A06800	#B57600	#C98300	#DC9000	#EF9C00
#3C0005	#560007	#6C000A	#820010	#960014	#A90017	#BC001D	#CF0021	#DF0024
#3D0011	#57001A	#6E0023	#83002C	#980034	#AB003C	#BD0043	#D1004B	#E10052
#000000	#121212	#252525	#363636	#464646	#555555	#636363	#707070	#7D7D7D

#E62B86	#EA5493	#EE71A2	#F289AE	#F5A0BD	#F7B5CB	#F9C8D8	#FCDBE4	#FDEDF2
#9C2C86	#A74992	#B1629F	#BC7AAC	#C790B9	#D2A6C7	#DEBDD6	#E9D2E4	#F4E8F0
#4A2885	#5C3E90	#6F559D	#826BA9	#9781B7	#AA99C5	#BFB2D3	#D4CAE2	#EAE4EF
#2D73B9	#497FBF	#648DC7	#7C9BCF	#93A9D5	#AABADD	#C0CBE7	#D5DCEF	#EBECF6
#00AEED	#00B5EF	#49BDEF	#6EC6F1	#8DCFF4	#A5D8F6	#BFE2F9	#D4ECFB	#EBF5FC
#00A9A4	#00B1AE	#49BAB6	#6FC3C1	#8CCCCA	#A7D6D5	#BEE0DF	#D5EAE9	#EBF4F3
#00A54E	#00AD63	#3EB677	#69C08A	#89CA9D	#A4D4B0	#BEDFC4	#D5E9D7	#EBF4EA
#8DCB41	#9DD05B	#AED673	#BBDB88	#C7E19E	#D4E7B2	#E0EDC5	#EAF3DA	#F5F8EC
#FAF519	#FCF64C	#FEF76E	#FEF886	#FFF99D	#FFFAB2	#FFFBC6	#FFFDDA	#FFFDED
#F1A629	#F3B044	#F5BA5C	#F8C473	#FACD8A	#FBD7A1	#FDE2B8	#FDEBCF	#FFF5E8
#E3372E	#E7573B	#EB714D	#EF8861	#F39E77	#F6B28F	#FAC6AA	#FCD9C5	#FEEDE3
#E5325E	#E9556A	#ED717A	#F0888A	#F49F9C	#F6B3AD	#F9C7C2	#FCDAD5	#FEEDEA
#898989	#959595	#A0A0A0	#ACACAC	#B7B7B7	#C2C2C2	#CCCCCC	#D7D7D7	#ECECEC

extra bits

color codes p. 112

- You can also represent colors by specifying their red, green, and blue components either as a percentage or as a numerical value from 0–255. For example, to create our blue 4D65A0, you would use 30% red, 40% green and 63% blue. That could be written as rgb(30%, 40%, 63%) or as rgb(77, 101, 160) (since 77 is 30% of 255, etc). Nevertheless, the hexadecimal system is the most common.

- Hexadecimal means base 16. It is used commonly in computer programming. You can find a table of hexadecimal values on my web site: http://www.cookwood.com/ html/ in the extras section.

sixteen named colors p. 113

- There are other color names that some browsers will understand. The color names listed here are the names that all browsers will understand.

- Because the sixteen predefined colors are RGB colors—designed to be viewed on screen, rather than paper—they may look slightly different printed than they do on your monitor.

a selection of colors p. 114

- You can find this collection of colors (as well as the 16 predefined colors and a group of "web-safe" colors that are good for old monitors) on my web site: http:// www.cookwood.com/html/ in the extras section.

appendix d: symbols

In this appendix, you'll find a listing of the most common accented characters and special symbols, along with their code names (entities), as well as number references. The entities are perhaps easier to remember, but both systems are equally valid.

Note that the tables were generated with a browser, for authenticity's sake, and thus appear slightly more pixelated than regular text in this book.

symbols and characters

Characters with special meaning in html

Entity	Entity Displayed	Number	Number Displayed	Description
&	&	&	&	ampersand
>	>	>	>	greater-than sign
<	<	<	<	less-than sign
"	"	"	"	quotation mark = APL quote

Accented characters, accents, and other diacritics from Western European languages

Entity	Entity Displayed	Number	Number Displayed	Description
´	´	´	´	acute accent = spacing acute
¸	¸	¸	¸	cedilla = spacing cedilla
ˆ	^	ˆ	^	modifier letter circumflex accent
¯	¯	¯	¯	macron = spacing macron = overline = APL overbar
·	·	·	·	middle dot = Georgian comma = Greek middle dot
˜	˜	˜	˜	small tilde
¨	¨	¨	¨	diaeresis = spacing diaeresis
Á	Á	Á	Á	latin capital letter A with acute
á	á	á	á	latin small letter a with acute
Â	Â	Â	Â	latin capital letter A with circumflex
â	â	â	â	latin small letter a with circumflex
Æ	Æ	Æ	Æ	latin capital letter AE = latin capital ligature AE
æ	æ	æ	æ	latin small letter ae = latin small ligature ae
À	À	À	À	latin capital letter A with grave = latin capital letter A grave
à	à	à	à	latin small letter a with grave = latin small letter a grave
Å	Å	Å	Å	latin capital letter A with ring above = latin capital letter A ring
å	å	å	å	latin small letter a with ring above = latin small letter a ring
Ã	Ã	Ã	Ã	latin capital letter A with tilde
ã	ã	ã	ã	latin small letter a with tilde
Ä	Ä	Ä	Ä	latin capital letter A with diaeresis
ä	ä	ä	ä	latin small letter a with diaeresis
Ç	Ç	Ç	Ç	latin capital letter C with cedilla

Accented characters, accents, and other diacritics
from Western European languages (continued)

Entity	Entity Displayed	Number	Number Displayed	Description
&ccedil;	ç	&#231;	ç	latin small letter c with cedilla
&Eacute;	É	&#201;	É	latin capital letter E with acute
&eacute;	é	&#233;	é	latin small letter e with acute
&Ecirc;	Ê	&#202;	Ê	latin capital letter E with circumflex
&ecirc;	ê	&#234;	ê	latin small letter e with circumflex
&Egrave;	È	&#200;	È	latin capital letter E with grave
&egrave;	è	&#232;	è	latin small letter e with grave
&ETH;	Ð	&#208;	Ð	latin capital letter ETH
&eth;	ð	&#240;	ð	latin small letter eth
&Euml;	Ë	&#203;	Ë	latin capital letter E with diaeresis
&euml;	ë	&#235;	ë	latin small letter e with diaeresis
&Iacute;	Í	&#205;	Í	latin capital letter I with acute
&iacute;	í	&#237;	í	latin small letter i with acute
&Icirc;	Î	&#206;	Î	latin capital letter I with circumflex
&icirc;	î	&#238;	î	latin small letter i with circumflex
&Igrave;	Ì	&#204;	Ì	latin capital letter I with grave
&igrave;	ì	&#236;	ì	latin small letter i with grave
&Iuml;	Ï	&#207;	Ï	latin capital letter I with diaeresis
&iuml;	ï	&#239;	ï	latin small letter i with diaeresis
&Ntilde;	Ñ	&#209;	Ñ	latin capital letter N with tilde
&ntilde;	ñ	&#241;	ñ	latin small letter n with tilde
&Oacute;	Ó	&#211;	Ó	latin capital letter O with acute
&oacute;	ó	&#243;	ó	latin small letter o with acute
&Ocirc;	Ô	&#212;	Ô	latin capital letter O with circumflex
&ocirc;	ô	&#244;	ô	latin small letter o with circumflex
&OElig;	Œ	&#338;	Œ	latin capital ligature OE
&oelig;	œ	&#339;	œ	latin small ligature oe (note)
&Ograve;	Ò	&#210;	Ò	latin capital letter O with grave
&ograve;	ò	&#242;	ò	latin small letter o with grave
&Oslash;	Ø	&#216;	Ø	latin capital letter O with stroke = latin capital letter O slash
&oslash;	ø	&#248;	ø	latin small letter o with stroke, = latin small letter o slash

symbols and characters

Accented characters, accents, and other diacritics from Western European languages (continued)

Entity	Entity Displayed	Number	Number Displayed	Description
Õ	Õ	Õ	Õ	latin capital letter O with tilde
õ	õ	õ	õ	latin small letter o with tilde
Ö	Ö	Ö	Ö	latin capital letter O with diaeresis
ö	ö	ö	ö	latin small letter o with diaeresis
Š	Š	Š	Š	latin capital letter S with caron
š	š	š	š	latin small letter s with caron
ß	ß	ß	ß	latin small letter sharp s = ess-zed
Þ	Þ	Þ	Þ	latin capital letter THORN
þ	þ	þ	þ	latin small letter thorn
Ú	Ú	Ú	Ú	latin capital letter U with acute
ú	ú	ú	ú	latin small letter u with acute
Û	Û	Û	Û	latin capital letter U with circumflex
û	û	û	û	latin small letter u with circumflex
Ù	Ù	Ù	Ù	latin capital letter U with grave
ù	ù	ù	ù	latin small letter u with grave
Ü	Ü	Ü	Ü	latin capital letter U with diaeresis
ü	ü	ü	ü	latin small letter u with diaeresis
Ý	Ý	Ý	Ý	latin capital letter Y with acute
ý	ý	ý	ý	latin small letter y with acute
ÿ	ÿ	ÿ	ÿ	latin small letter y with diaeresis
Ÿ	Ÿ	Ÿ	Ÿ	latin capital letter Y with diaeresis

Currency characters

Entity	Entity Displayed	Number	Number Displayed	Description
¢	¢	¢	¢	cent sign
¤	¤	¤	¤	currency sign
€	€	€	€	euro sign
£	£	£	£	pound sign
¥	¥	¥	¥	yen sign = yuan sign

Punctuation

Entity	Entity Displayed	Number	Number Displayed	Description
¦	¦	¦	¦	broken bar = broken vertical bar
•	•	•	•	bullet = black small circle (note)
©	©	©	©	copyright sign
†	†	†	†	dagger
‡	‡	‡	‡	double dagger
⁄	/	⁄	/	fraction slash
…	...	…	...	horizontal ellipsis = three dot leader
¡	¡	¡	¡	inverted exclamation mark
ℑ	ℑ	ℑ	ℑ	blackletter capital I = imaginary part
¿	¿	¿	¿	inverted question mark = turned question mark
‎		‎		left-to-right mark (for formatting only)
—	—	—	—	em dash
–	–	–	–	en dash
¬	¬	¬	¬	not sign
‾	‾	‾	‾	overline = spacing overscore
ª	ª	ª	ª	feminine ordinal indicator
º	º	º	º	masculine ordinal indicator
¶	¶	¶	¶	pilcrow sign = paragraph sign
‰	‰	‰	‰	per mille sign
′	′	′	′	prime = minutes = feet
″	″	″	″	double prime = seconds = inches
ℜ	ℜ	ℜ	ℜ	blackletter capital R = real part symbol
®	®	®	®	registered sign = registered trade mark sign
‏		‏		right-to-left mark (for formatting only)
§	§	§	§	section sign
­		­		soft hyphen = discretionary hyphen (displays incorrectly on Mac)
¹	¹	¹	¹	superscript one = superscript digit one
™	™	™	™	trade mark sign
℘	℘	℘	℘	script capital P = power set = Weierstrass p

symbols and characters

Punctuation (continued)

Entity	Entity Displayed	Number	Number Displayed	Description
&bdquo;	„	&#8222;	„	double low-9 quotation mark
&laquo;	«	&#171;	«	left-pointing double angle quotation mark = left pointing guillemet
&ldquo;	"	&#8220;	"	left double quotation mark
&lsaquo;	‹	&#8249;	‹	single left-pointing angle quotation mark (note)
&lsquo;	'	&#8216;	'	left single quotation mark
&raquo;	»	&#187;	»	right-pointing double angle quotation mark = right pointing guillemet
&rdquo;	"	&#8221;	"	right double quotation mark
&rsaquo;	›	&#8250;	›	single right-pointing angle quotation mark (note)
&rsquo;	'	&#8217;	'	right single quotation mark
&sbquo;	,	&#8218;	,	single low-9 quotation mark
				em space
				en space
				no-break space = non-breaking space
				thin space
&zwj;		&#8205;		zero width joiner
&zwnj;		&#8204;		zero width non-joiner

Mathematical symbols

Entity	Entity Displayed	Number	Number Displayed	Description
&deg;	°	&#176;	°	degree sign
&divide;	÷	&#247;	÷	division sign
&frac12;	$\frac{1}{2}$	&#189;	$\frac{1}{2}$	vulgar fraction one half = fraction one half
&frac14;	$\frac{1}{4}$	&#188;	$\frac{1}{4}$	vulgar fraction one quarter = fraction one quarter
&frac34;	$\frac{3}{4}$	&#190;	$\frac{3}{4}$	vulgar fraction three quarters = fraction three quarters
&ge;	≥	&#8805;	≥	greater-than or equal to
&le;	≤	&#8804;	≤	less-than or equal to
&minus;	−	&#8722;	−	minus sign
&sup2;	^{2}	&#178;	^{2}	superscript two = superscript digit two = squared
&sup3;	^{3}	&#179;	^{3}	superscript three = superscript digit three = cubed
&times;	×	&#215;	×	multiplication sign

index

index

index

index